Wall Street Wonders

Sheldon Zerden

DEDICATION

A word of thanks to my triple inspiration

Charlotte, Judith, and Deborah.

CONTENTS

ACKNOWLEDGMENTS

"Nothing so evil as money ever grew to be current among men."

- Euripides

PREFACE

One of the most exciting aspects of life today is the keen interest people are showing in the stock market. Of course, the drive behind this popularity is the lure of money… the pot of gold at the end of the rainbow.

Today's society is saturated with materialism and luxury. It is natural that the have-nots hope to attain a higher standard of living.

This substantial middle class group is flocking in growing numbers to the promised land of Wall street… the utopia, their friends tell them, where money multiplies overnight.

In many cases the want of luxury turns to greed, and eventually to tragedy.

1) A NEW STATUS SYMBOL

The consistent rise in the number of investors during the last ten years has established the following facts: that stock ownership has reached a new level of respectability, that the fear of the depression of the 1930s has been dissipated, and that the ownership of shares of stock in a corporation has become one of our many symbols of status.

The awe which the sacred inner sanctum of branch offices of brokerage houses held for the average person has now been replaced by the mass fascination of watching an enlarged version of ticker tape dance by, with symbols of the various companies announcing the latest prices as each trade is transacted.

This intriguing tape watching has achieved such an advanced state of hypnotic concentration with the public that is not impossible to see a person bump his head on the exit door while walking backwards, and catching a last, lingering look at the moving quotations.

Market behavior is usually measured by several groups of averages. The most prominent of these are the Dow Jones Averages, which recently have been breaking all past records. These yardsticks have become very important to investors and speculators alike, for it is by means of these averages that one immediately knows whether there is a good or bad day in the market.

A little anecdote that is told in reference to the above is about an old man who owns ten shares of Studebaker. He patronizes one particular office every day for part of his lunch hour. Each time he enters the office he inquires,

"How is the Dow Jones averages?"

We all know that the Dow Jones Averages have no direct bearing on the action of his stock, but its chances are better if the key stocks in the industrial average are making a spirited move. So... do not laugh at the old man or his remark. Those ten shares that he owns are very important to him, and the averages may help buoy his stock to a point where he can sell and realize a profit.

That brings us to the "raison d'etre" for the stock market and the many exchanges which trade in their shares. Companies are in business to make a profit. People buy common stocks for the same reason.

Shares of stock in thousands of corporations are traded on various exchanges. The foremost of these is the New York Stock Exchange, which trades in the shares of over fifteen hundred companies. Thousands of others are traded in the over-the-counter market, and are not subject to certain rules such as minimum shares, periodic reporting of profit and loss. It is this lack of public knowledge of inside dealings which the Securities and Exchange Commission brought out in its latest report.

The profit motive and the desire for monetary gain are common to us all, and it is for this purpose that we risk our money. it is a fact that regardless of the quality of the stock you buy, when you lay your money on the line, there is always an element of risk. Once you've digested this bit of truth you can proceed to place your money in companies which offer growth, income, or speculative appeal.

Here I am reminded of a classic bit of dialogue between an investor and a speculator. A man meets his friend in the street, and after the amenities and the pleasantries of everyday meeting, he gets down to the important talk such as how each is doing in the stock market. One says to the other,

"Say, tell me Jack, are you an investor or a speculator?

"I'll tell you no lie, Tom, I started out as a speculator, and the stock I bought went down, and now I'm an investor!"

The reality of this discussion refers to the fact that a speculator buys and sells often, whereas an investor usually holds an issue for a longer period.

There is also a lesson to be learned from the stoic acceptance on Jack's part that his stock went down, and this fact made him an investor. As a trader or a speculator Jack should have sold his stock as soon as it started to fall.

2) GROWTH STOCK

In the wide spectrum of the investment world there is no soul-satisfying experience to compare with the ownership of an outstanding growth stock. There is never a guarantee of profit in the stock market, but because of their consistent record of increased sales and earnings, growth stocks provide the key to a true compounding of a person's money.

If the surest way to have your money grow is to buy growth stocks, why don't all stockholders buy them in preference to the other kinds of common stocks? The answer in part is this: for people who are advanced in years, and have to get a fair dividend return on their invested capital to augment their income, growth stocks are not the answer, The yields on most growth equities are very low, and for good reason. For those who still cling to the fear that a high price earnings ratio is to be avoided at all costs, growth issues are not their cup of tea. Most growth stocks have been chased up in piece to the point where their price earnings ratios are high. Finally, for those who like to buy round lots, so they can tell their friends they own 300 shares of this and 200 shares of that... growth stocks are not for them. Most growth stocks are in the high priced category.

Price to earnings buffs, income seekers, and round lot addicts make up a large segment of the investing public. It should now be clear why all investors don't want growth stocks. The disadvantage of owning these low-dividend- paying, high priced, high price to earnings ratio stocks would seem to negate the advantages of their predicted growth. Let me see why, despite the obvious disadvantages, many people continue to flock to the growth banner.

For one thing, no company can grow without increasing its sales and earnings. That is why all growth companies continue to expand. In order to expand it is necessary to use earnings for research and development. This research discovers new products, which in turn creates the need for new plants. All the while, sales keep increasing. Instead of paying out earnings in the form of dividends those companies plow money back into expansion.

A price to earnings ratio is not static, and an aggressive growth company can shrink that ratio with amazing rapidity. The excuse for not buying a growth stock is a very weak one. The high prices which growth stocks usually command should not be a deterrent to their purchase. One will find that the high pieces generally continue to get higher and higher.

For those fortunate investors who own International Business Machines, Litton industries, Xerox, Bristol Myers, Polaroid, and a host of others. The rewards of buying growth are brought home clearly with each upward move. The pleasure comes from the knowledge of the importance which each company maintains in its own field. They are prime movers ... they create new products... they even form new industries.

The highest tribute that can be paid to them is that their excellence is not only constantly on the tongues of their stockholders, but grudgingly, and in unbelievable amazement by those who continue to find excuses for not buying them.

3) YOU CAN'T GO BROKE TAKING A PROFIT

One of the most difficult decisions to make in the market is when to take a profit. When a person is lucky enough to have a winner (and I use the word lucky advisedly), he immediately envisions himself riding high on a gold-braided palanquin, being fanned with ostrich feathers by Nubian slaves. This picture is only a symbol of the unreal, imaginary world which greed can produce.

The reality of a fluctuating market can bring such a reverie to a quick and unceremonious end. Market values build up and dissipate very quickly. People who have profit in any stock act very slowly in most instances, and many times their hesitation can result in the loss of the entire profit which they may have realized.

Some brokers say a fair profit for a short term transaction should be 10% of the investment. Whether or not that is sufficient is a matter for personal or individual decision. When confronted with such a pleasurable task, it is best to decide and act with celerity. When you have sold a stock it is wise to try to forget about it, for if it continues to rise as is the case when YOU sell, it can lead to unhappiness, nervousness, and recriminations. The fact remains that a profit was made, and Lord knows that is better than a loss. Try to reinvest the funds in something which is just as good or better than the one you've just sold.

All too often a person with a large profit is reluctant to sell and a bear market can nullify years of rising prices. There is no set formula for market timing, but experts agree that it is the key to success in investing. It is also very important to know which stocks to hold for the long pull and which to sell for a short term profit. Careful management of a portfolio can mean the difference. So, before you plan the safari or the beach house in the Virgin Islands, start cleaning out the dead wood and revise those stocks. The warm winds are beckoning.

4) AVERAGING YOUR WAY TO THE POOR HOUSE

People who put their money in the stock market usually do so with the full realization that they may lose all or part of it. The thought of losing hard-earned money is always easier to take than the reality. If a person buys a stock and sees it go down, he invariably starts to find reasons why it has happened. He rationalizes.. the market is bad... the news of the merger has not been spread around yet... the earnings are going to be good, so I'll wait another few weeks. These and many other reasons lull the unlucky person into a trance of indecision. After an extended period of time the stock has not snapped back, and the market is good. The merger is off, the earnings are reported and they are bad. What could be worse than all that adverse publicity! All the bad news is out. Instead of selling and retaining the major portion of his principle, our wishful thinking stockholder does the worst thing he could under the circumstances... he buys more of the same stock. This action is called averaging out. He had purchased the original stock at ten dollars a share, so when he buys an equal amount at five dollars a share his average price will be only seven and one-half dollars.

All would be well if the stock had the slightest intention of going up. The trouble is that even during a good market, a Bull Market, the good stocks go up and the bad ones go down. This particular stock has already spent a year proving that it is a bad one.

To bring this sad story to its unfortunate conclusion, the stock continues to go down, and our stockholder begins to experience all the painful consequences of losing money. He daydreams, he finds it hard to go to sleep at night... he just stares at the ceiling. If his wife happens to know about his misadventure with this stock, his life is plagued with innuendoes and constant nagging.

Finally, in desperation, our stockholder is jolted out of his lethargy, and at two dollars a share he sells the stock. The cancer is finally removed, and a year of nightmares is ended. A sadder but wiser person, our friend is free of the fear of further loss from his stock. He will have learned a bitter lesson which can have important consequences for his future in the stock market... provided his memory is good.

5) COMPANY MOTTOS

During the frenzy which attended the electronic boom of the 1950s, it became psychologically important for a company to have a corporate name that had some electronic sounding ending. Name endings were changed and new ones added with reckless abandon. New issues with technical names doubled in price on the day of their issue. This was not because of the merit of the company's business outlook, but rather the fact that the name indicated a relation to the booming electronic industry.

Many new investors were buying stocks without inquiring about the past record, earnings potential, or knowing the product lines of the companies involved. Speculators, encouraged by quick success in such trades, were doing the same.

From an investment point of view this method of buying stock is not only inexcusable it is against every rule in the book. Even with a speculation, some caution should be exercised, and a knowledge of the company and its prospects should be known. An illustration of this blind purchase of a company is graphically presented in the following dialogue :

"I told you – you wouldn't listen. That stock is going all the way."

"What do you mean?"

"You heard me...all the way...I bought it At 4 ½. It's already at 10 and still looking smart."

"What makes you think it's going to keep going up?"

"It can't miss!"

"Yes, but you don't understand. Do you realize how many swimming pools are sold in this country every year?
And not only that, they have a terrific backlog!"

"Swimming pools? Yeah, that's a terrific business... I think I'll buy one hundred shares. Say, you got me so hepped up you didn't even tell me the name of the stock!"

"Aqua filter. It's over-the-counter."

FACT: Aqua filter OTC –main source of income....cigarette filters.

Overheard in the board room...

"Boy, have I got a winner...not that I want to boast."

"What's the name, if I'm not too inquisitive?"

"New Haven Clock, it's on the American Stock Exchange."

"What do they do?

"They're an old company somewhere in Connecticut, Hartford, I think. They are in electronics. They have a lot of defense business."

"Do you think it's a good time to buy it now?
"Sure, it's bound to have a new spurt with all the new defense spending."

FACT: New Haven Clock is located in Florida and deals in real estate.

More care is necessary in buying stock today. Selectivity has returned to the market, and a company's name is only as good as its corporate history, current earnings, and its future potential. With those credentials, to paraphrase the immortal Shakespeare... no rose could smell as sweet regardless of the name

6) "I'VE MISSED THE BOAT"

There is an old saying on the "Street" that goes…. "I've missed the Boat." It simply means that a stock has had an extended run up and as usual, you have not bought it. The common expression of regret is, "I'm not going to chase after it!" This situation has happened time and time again with many good growth stocks and special situations. International Business machines, Minnesota Mining, American Home Products, Polaroid, and Revlon, to name a few companies which have had spirited moves, and millions of people who watch the market were aware of it. In fact, some of these stocks are still making their moves!.

As long as the expression includes the word boat, I am tempted to analogize with the image of a lovely cruise ship. It is wonderful to be on one of those lovely liners when it makes its way through the warm sunshine of the Caribbean. The nights are cool and the days are sunny. The reality of this analogy is that the ship must return to its home port. Then there is an opportunity for many more fortunate people to board the liner for another delightful trip to paradise. This pleasure steamer returns again and again, always willing to to accept new passengers. The crew is the same, the food is just as delicious, and the ports of call are identical. The only difference is that you are there to relish the advantages which such a ship can offer.

If the comparison seems far-fetched, just explore your memory and recall how silly you felt when you cancelled that order for Fairchild Camera at 28 ½ and saw it run all the way up to 260. How many people have remarked about International Business Machines, "It's much too high!" That stock will always be too high. How often have people followed the ascent of a Polaroid or a Xerox with stunned fascination and failed to do anything but shake their heads in amazement.

"How high can Litton go" asked one bewildered investor.

"How high is up?" answered another, with an equal amount of perplexity.

The moral is very clear, or it should be. No one has missed the "boat". It's still there... and so are the rewards for those who want to come aboard.

7) PORTFOLIO BUILDING

One of the cardinal principles of sound investing is to have a diversified portfolio. The usual tragedy for most people is that they have far less than one can consider a portfolio, and that their diversified group of stocks is nothing but a hodge podge of stocks which have been accumulated through the years upon the advice of well-intentioned friends, hot tips which have cooled off, and unsuccessful hunches. It is difficult to understand the inertia which paralyzes investors whose money has lain dormant in inactive stocks. They sit idly by and painfully watch the new favorites capture the headlines every day. If a stock does not perform in a reasonable period of time... sell it and put the money into something else. Most people are reluctant to take a loss. They wait an unlimited amount of time in an attempt to recover every nickel of their investment. This is a mistake. The loss of time could prove valuable in another stock... one which in the process of making a spectacular move.

The essentials of a person's objective should change with his age. The following recommendations offer in a general way a portfolio plan for the various investors:

The average mix of holdings for a young man should be strongly weighted with growth stocks. It should include some income producers for new investment reserves, and a small percentage of quality stocks with the potential for capital appreciation.

The middle-aged person,, man or woman, should retain about half of his or her money in quality growth issues. The other half should be in income stocks, safe blue chips, and defensive issues. Speculative stocks in these portfolios should be left up to the individual.

When a person reaches retirement age he should be interested in income and safety. He can't afford to risk his money. He needs all the income he can get to supplement his social security and other forms of income. For this group of investors no growth stocks are recommended because few growth stocks offer income. For the most part the utilities, tobaccos, food stocks, and other defensive issues should make up these portfolios. No speculation is called for. The balance of the investment should consist of dividend paying blue chips.

This is a brief review of the average requirements for persons in the various groups of investors. It should be understood that there are always exceptions in individual cases. These problems are the responsibility of the registered representative if he is the sole custodian and advisor of an investor. The goals should be decided at the outset, and when an investor strays from his objective he should be cautioned by his broker.

The adoption of a well-planned program by an investor and a registered representative, and the strict adherence to its step-by-step execution, is the intelligent way to a successful foray into the stock market. Without a professionally planned beginning and a periodic revision and weeding of your stock garden, you can't seriously expect to have more than that same potpourri, to which people facetiously refer as your "well diversified portfolio."

8) HOT TIPS

The hot tip is the bane of the stock market. The fact that it is usually the tip which launches people on their stock market way is less vital than the truth in most cases. The tip is the product of a rumor which usually fizzles.

Customers' men make a living by buying and selling stock. When you come to them with a stock purchase in mind, they will caution you if it is too speculative in nature. All too often, however, your burning enthusiasm is fired by greed and it is too powerful to be overcome by a cool judgment on the part opf your broker. The admonition should contain a proviso making it urgent to review the stock shortly after its purchase. If the heat which created the enthusiasm has waned, (and a drop in the price of the stock causes that) then you should be man enough to realize your error, take your loss, and find another stock for your money. Hesitancy causes greater losses.

There is no law which says that all tips are no good. Some work out well. But beware of tips received from strangers and people too closely involved with a particular firm. They may have a reason for wanting people to buy the stock. It may be that they want to sell it. There is no harm in accepting bona fide information about a company and acting with alacrity to make use of the news. Firstly, ask a broker's opinion... secondly, learn all you can about the company's past record and current situation. If you are satisfied that all is well, buy the stock. If the startling news which tempted you to buy doesn't cause the stock to move, get out as fast as you can. There are other stocks which are moving.

Tips, rumors, gossip, mergers, increased dividends, stock splits, and new products are the ingredients in the recipe of everyday's market cake. These news items are the active force behind the market's action. If one has inside news before the public, he must realize a profit. But once the news is released the stock, which has risen in anticipation of the news, usually goes down. It does so because "the news is out."

So chart your course carefully, investigate thoroughly, and let someone else learn by sad experience. Learn vicariously and don't let tips mislead you. Use them wisely to your advantage in an intelligent and reasoning attempt to show a profit in the stock market.

9) THOSE QUIET SENTINELS OF WALL STREET

Throughout the last fifteen years, when stock ownership tripled from 7 million to 20 million, the unsung heroes of the boardroom have withstood the tide of growth and change with laudable aplomb.

Even before the current era, when the buying of stock has assumed mass proportions, these gentlemen lent distinction to a professional calling which marked a furious and hysterical bedlam that the public would find hard to understand.

These men advise and guide their customers through the maze of financial data and gossip, and it is their responsibility to help in avoiding the pitfalls of haphazard investing.

A conscientious young man on such a job not only finds it important to do many hours of research, but in his attempt to grow on the job would also consider it his duty to devote much of his spare time to reading the mountains of reports, magazines, and statistical services. In this way our broker will be adding to his stature, and improving his ability to provide his customers with a maximum of adequate service.

Since he is constantly handling other peoples' money, it is imperative that the honesty, character, and integrity of the financial advisor be above reproach. One cannot expect the usually intelligent investor to be gullible enough to be misled for too long by a dishonest or expedient operator.

There have been cases of unethical and immoral brokers, but the policing of the Securities and Exchange Commission since 1933 keeps the incidence down to an infinitesimal minimum. Those who resort to shady dealings find that their mistakes return to haunt them. They are usually unceremoniously drummed out of the business.

There are many persons in this field who gain their success through inheritance. Others enjoy healthy income because they have an affluent coterie of friends and relatives. The majority of men, however, must depend on their personality, intelligence, and an unrelenting effort to acquire new accounts, and to keep from losing them.

The fascinating middlemen of the boardrooms are the face which Wall Street proudly shows the public. They set the standards that make the market for billions of dollars of assets. They man the trading block of thousands of companies large and small which comprise our free economy. Their efforts to foretell the future do not always succeed…. Don't judge them too harshly… theirs is no bed of roses. They alternate between elation and despair, and although the boardroom is their home, the world is their arena. Their collective integrity redounds to the greatness of their chosen profession… those quit sentinels of Wall Street.

10) FUNDS OR STOCKS
CONCENTRATION VERSUS DIVERSIFICATION

A raging controversy which has occupied investment circles for years is whether a mutual fund is a better form of investment than any assorted hand-picked group of stocks. While this question was being debated, sales of both funds and stocks continued to make and break new records.

Mutual funds are not a new form of investment. There are records of funds which go back to the early 1920s, and even before then. As the years progressed, funds became more and more popular. People realized that as the owner of a fund they could be part of a massive buying and earning power, have an undreamed of diversification for an almost minute investment, and finally they learned that with the constant day to day management, they were provided with a safety factor not found in their ordinary investment relationship.

People who bought funds in the early days have reaped the harvest of solid growth in value. Due to the safety of a diversified portfolio, however, the dilution of growth was bound to be a factor. These people had long since forgotten that they had paid a substantial fee for the purchase and subsequent management of the fund.

Today, many funds have added low cost insurance, which insures a widow of a paid up ten year mutual fund plan.

The disadvantages of a mutual fund are concisely: a loading charge or sales charge is usually eight percent or more. This charge does not include a custodian fee, life insurance fee, and other charges. Growth is not guaranteed but still depends on the action of the stocks owned by the fund. This growth is usually gradual due to the wide diversification which usually includes the stable and slow moving utilities, preferred stocks, and the rock-bound safety of fixed income bonds. The types of funds have been growing, and there is now a fund for almost every objective. The one which was described was a balanced fund. The late 1950s saw the emergence of growth funds, and this led to the daring performance funds with their active trading in the glamour favorites. The latest funds which are now coming out are the dual funds which give the investor a choice of growth or income. There are also many no-load funds which have no salesman and therefore no sales charge. Those funds which do have a sales charge bring us to the main objection to mutual funds. All charges of a fund are deducted from the payments received in the first few purchases. If one should happen to need money in the first year or two after his investment in a mutual fund, he would find that the value of his investment, less than the amount of charges deducted, would be below his original cost. A fund should be considered a long term investment. The front-end load as it is called is the biggest complaint which the Securities and Exchange Commission found in its report on the mutual fund industry..

On the plus side, it must be understood that a mutual fund is an investment which has tremendous resources behind it. Fresh money is constantly coming in, and it can therefore take advantage of new buying opportunities. It can give a person with limited funds, in some cases as little as ten dollars a month, a stake in a diversified list of investments. Its management is constantly alert for opportunities to switch out of bad stocks and into promising ones for the benefit of all the shareholders. Professional management and constant supervision is what you are buying when you own a fund, and the safety of diversification as well. It is also a good point to remember that the S.E.C. concluded in its report with a statement which in effect stated that the growth of the mutual fund industry has shown that there is a great deal to be said for the successful record of many small investors who could otherwise nit safely invest their money in individual stocks because of the small amount of capital at their disposal.

With the many features a fund offers it would seem an ideal area for millions of new investors to place their money. No doubt many new people have done just that. Without a thorough knowledge of the stock market they thought it would be wise to leave the decisions of investing up to the experts. The growth of mutual funds from 500 million dollars in assets in 1946 to 38 billion dollars in assets in 1967 attests to their popularity and success, and this was so stated in the S.E.C. report.

On the other hand there are millions of investors who will settle for nothing less than the pride of ownership. They identify with the company they buy. They buy its products whenever possible. They relish the certificate which declares that they own a share of a corporation, and cry aloud when it is late in being transferred into their name. These sophisticated investors deplore what they consider to be an exorbitant charge for the purchase of a fund. They would rather pick their own stocks with the help of a broker. There is no possibility of dilution when a stock is bought by an individual and it starts going up. The appreciation can be realized. It is also true that in the event of a loss, and there are many of these cases, the full weight of the loss is suffered by the stockholder.

The success stories which lay at the source of many

investors' attempts in the stock market, drive them to look for the one sleeper which will make them rich. This urge to be rich cannot be fulfilled with the purchase of a fund, although you can achieve a compounding of your investment. There are many cases of fortunate people who have become millionaires by concentrating in one stock. The sustained drive of this stock along with stock splits and a continued rise can compound an investment in a relatively short period of years into a fortune. This urge for money can only be realized in the quick, exciting action of individual stocks. Of course this method can often lead to tragedy. Stocks and the market go both ways, and in 1962, 1966, 1987, and 2008 the stock market plunged dramatically and fortunes were lost.

No doubt the controversy about mutual funds and individual stocks will go on and on. And certainly both will be bought heavily in the exciting years to come. Those who want safety and a conservative investment without the headaches of buying and selling will buy the funds. Those with daring and adventure will accept the challenge of the stock market. They will educate themselves to the point of sophistication, and with the knowledge they have accumulated they will proceed to forge the decisions which they hope will lead them to the promised land of pleasure, prestige, and success.

11 MARKET AXIOMS

There is a market axiom for just about every situation. Among the most famous are J.P. Morgan's , "The market will fluctuate," and Rothschild's "I buy sheep and sell dear."

As in all aphorisms, whether they are about religion, marriage, philosophy, or any other branch of knowledge. Some are contradictory and others misleading. They have, however, found their way into the folklore of the stock market, and here courtesy of Leffler, is a compilation of some of the better known market expressions.

When to buy and sell is more important than what to buy and sell.

Don't rely on the advice of the insiders.

Cut losses and let profits run.

Sell when the good news is out.

Never quarrel with the tape.

There is no need to always be in the market.

Never put a halo around a stock.

Avoid too frequent switching.

The stock market has no past.

Never speculate for a special need.

Don't try to get the last eighth.

No one ever went broke taking profits.

A bull can make money in Wall Street; a bear can make money in Wall Street; but a hog never can.

Buy when others sell; sell when others buy.

Sell on the first margin call.

A margin call is the only sure tip from a broker.

Put half your profits in a safety deposit box.

Never buy a stock after a long decline.

Never answer a margin call.

Many a healthy reaction has proven fatal.

Never sell on strike news.

Stocks look best at the top of a bull market and worst at the bottom of a bear market.

It is not the price you pay for a stock, but the time you buy it that counts.

When in doubt, do nothing.

Learn to take a loss quickly.

Don't buy an egg until it is laid.

When prices close strong, after an all-day advance, the next move is generally downward.

Stocks which have the longest preceding advances have the longest declines.

All stocks move more or less with the general market, but value will tell in the long run.

Value has little to do with the temporary fluctuations in stock prices.

Beware of one who has nothing to lose.

The public is always wrong.

If you would not buy a stock, sell it.

Cut back your stocks to the sleeping point.

The market will continue to fluctuate.

An investor is just a disappointed speculator.

12) KEEPING A BUYING RESERVE

One of the most important tenets of the faith on Wall Street which is consistently ignored, is the requirement for keeping a buying reserve. The failure to adhere to this rule has achieved a universal feeling of disgust and self-guilt since shareholders are almost unanimous in their negligence. Saving a percentage of one's total resources is a sound method of preventing an investor from being helpless when an opportunity of unusual merit presents itself.

Of course there is a chance to escape the consequence of being fully bought up. The ability to take a loss would prevent a stockholder from being "locked in." The benefits of such a reality would be a boon to investors and financial advisors alike. The broker would increase his business and the customer would release a quantity of money for a new chance of making a profit.

This is one of the many theories which make the road to market profit sound easy. The only fly in the ointment is that people are people. They are guided by their emotions rather than a cold set of rules. It is easy to advise someone to take a loss, but difficult to take one yourself. Losing money comes hard, especially when there is the slightest amount of hope that a stock may come back.

The best advice for those investors who can't cold-bloodedly take a loss is to buy nothing but top grade stocks. Buy the quality company in each industry. If you happen to be unfortunate enough to buy at the start of a recession, and you find your stock gradually headed for oblivion, don't fret... even though you haven't the courage to sell at a loss, the business cycle will work in your favor. Have patience, and the surging economy during the recovery will carry your quality stocks back to their former levels. It is not so with stocks of inferior quality. In fact, a bad recession can mean the end for a small and unsound company.

The lesson should be clear. There is rarely a man with the desire to take a loss, even if it is for his own benefit. Therefore, to insure yourself a constant ability to take advantage of buying opportunities, make certain there is always a reserve available. Your broker should always know your financial situation so he can guide you properly. Take profits, buy your specialties but don't break the rule of keeping a reserve. Set the amount yourself. Be liquid... it shouldn't be 25 percent as some experts say at various times. Reach a new level of maturity as an intelligent investor. Save your sympathy for your friends who are "locked in." You have an extra set of keys, and open the door to opportunity.

13) STOCK SPLITS

A common misconception which is held by countless
thousands of stockholders is that a stock split in some
immediate way increases the value of one's holding.
The fact is simply that the amount of shares is increased
by the dimension of the split. In a two-for-one split, a
stockholder receives two shares for every one; in a
three-for-one split, he receives three shares for every
one, etc. In a two-for-one split for example, a
shareowner who owns one share art one hundred
dollars a share will then own two shares at fifty dollars a
share. There is no magic or miraculous doubling of one's
profit, as some people erroneously believe.

The rash of splits which paralleled the growth of
American Industry in the last decade has added many
millions of shares of stock for which there was a ready
market. Some companies issue shares for the purpose
of new acquisitions. Others with many consumer
products are happy to broaden their base of ownership.
They reason that the many new stockholders they add
when the price of the stock is split will buy their
products as loyal shareowners should, thus creating new
business.

In the majority of cases, the splitting of a stock follows a period of progress which starts with a rise in earnings and is followed by a surge in the price of the stock. If Newton's law of motion follows, "A body in motion tends to stay in motion," one can expect a continued rise in price of a stock, after the split takes place. This explains why the price of a stock rises very quickly after a stock split is announced. Many times the board of directors gives impetus to this continued rise by adding a dividend increase on the new stock.

It is an obvious fact that a stock split does have several advantages for its stockholders; it is the traditional way for long term investors to compound their capital gains. After the split, the growth of a good company will in time return to the original price at the time of the split. This would double the value of the investment. Assuming another split takes place years later and continued growth once again brings the price back to the old level, our stockholder now has four times his original investment. If the original investment was five thousand dollars, it would now be worth twenty thousand dollars.

A split brings the price of a stock down to a reasonable level, where the majority of investors can trade in round lots. That means they can buy one hundred shares at a time. One of the foremost exceptions to this fact is the high-priced Xerox Corporation which has always sold at high multiples. In 1962 Xerox was selling as low as 89 dollars a share. The next few years saw the stock reach a historic high of 400 dollars a share. It then split its stock 5 for 1. That means the shareholders received five new shares for every one they held. The new split stock started trading at 80 or so and it moved up to 270 or the equivalent of 1,350 dollars a share.

The rewards of the stock split are among the many incentives of investing. The road to wealth is marked with the splits of aggressive and growing companies. Their growth is reflected in an eager attempt by stockholders to purchase the company's stock. This demand causes the increase in the price of the stock. Those who hold on for the long pull gain the benefit of compound growth. Ironically enough, so do the people who thought that they doubled their money when the stock split two-for-one.

14) SELL, BUY OR HOLD

A dilemma of aggravating proportions presents itself to the stockholder with a paper loss. The fear that he has a loss is bad enough, but the problem of selecting a course of action is even more tantalizing. This type of decision is almost in a constant state of resolution, since there are very few investors who have profits in all their holdings.

There are three things a person can do. Firstly, he can sell the stock and establish a tax loss. In order to avail himself of the loss, he cannot repurchase the same stock before thirty-one days have passed. If he does, it would be a wash sale, and he would not be entitled to the loss. Secondly, he can hold the stock and hope that it will come back to the price level of its purchase or even higher. This is the helpless inertia of which plagues most stockholders. This is not a course of action, but is purely inaction. The stocks with paper losses in the portfolios of millions of investors have helped to immobilize their funds and have reduced those investors activity to the point of stagnation.

Lastly, there is an option on the part of the stockholder who remains loyal to the corporation whose stock he has bought, to add to his holding and at the same time reduce the average price at which the total amount of stock is owned. This is called "averaging down" or "averaging out." The down and out is purely a coincidence, and not intended as a pun. Let us see how the averaging out process works. Here is a simple example.

A dilemma of aggravating proportions presents itself to the stockholder with a paper loss. The fear that he has a loss is bad enough, but the problem of selecting a course of action is even more tantalizing. This type of decision is almost in a constant state of resolution, since there are very few investors who have profits in all their holdings.

There are three things a person can do. Firstly, he can sell the stock and establish a tax loss. In order to avail himself of the loss, he cannot repurchase the same stock before thirty-one days have passed. If he does, it would be a wash sale, and he would not be entitled to the loss. Secondly, he can hold the stock and hope that it will come back to the price level of its purchase or even higher. This is the helpless inertia of which plagues most stockholders. This is not a course of action, but is purely inaction. The stocks with paper losses in the portfolios of millions of investors have helped to immobilize their funds and have reduced those investors activity to the point of stagnation.

Lastly, there is an option on the part of the stockholder who remains loyal to the corporation whose stock he has bought, to add to his holding and at the same time reduce the average price at which the total amount of stock is owned. This is called "averaging down" or "averaging out." The down and out is purely a coincidence, and not intended as a pun. Let us see how the averaging out process works. Here is a simple example.

15) MONEY

Twenty-five years ago, the Greek playwright Euripides said, "Nothing so evil as money ever grew to be current among men." This was during the flourishing era of Greece which marked the beginning of recorded literature. Today, twenty-five centuries later, the pursuit of money has not waned, but has increased in intensity, until the preoccupation with money has approached the level of hysteria.

Envy, jealousy, and crimes of every description are caused by the desire for money. Immorality, bribery, embezzlement, and other degrading human actions are committed in its quest. In addition, one of the biggest businesses in the country is gambling, whether it's the horses, roulette table, trotters, a state lottery, or the dog track. Everybody loves money and tries to find new ways to acquire it. It seems that the only people who rationalize that money is not important are those who unfortunately don't have enough!

Lately, many millions of new people are discovering that the stock market offers opportunities for making money. Not as a sure thing, as friends of these new investors sometimes imply, but as a legal, and prestige-producing experience. Let us examine a cross section of these new additions to the stock market family.

Many young people with limited funds wisely choose a mutual fund. This is a safe way to have your money grow. Others with more funds may buy an individual stock which they expect will give them a reasonable return, and at the same time increase in value. Too many others of our new stockholders are entering the market with unfounded tips. Despite all the precautionary advertising by well-meaning brokerage houses and the New York Stock Exchange, still invest money which they need for the necessities of daily living and take unwise risks.

The lure of riches is so powerful that it can overcome the warnings of close friends, strangers, and experienced investors. Each person with a dream of success is deaf to the exhortations of doom by others. He enters a world of fantasy which is so real that he can actually taste the champagne! By the time the reverie is over, the tattered vestige of a hopeful investment no longer can support our dreamer in his present mode of life.

There should be no sympathy for a fool... one who bets his dinner money and loses. Even a gambler would agree. It is more to the point to understand how much grief bad investments can have on a family. The loss of money can become incidental, and a marital conflict may be the consequence.

This warning should be taken only as a caution against extremism. People should understand that money in itself is not bad. It is normal to like money and the things it can buy. It is necessary, however, to keep the importance of money in its proper perspective to the more abiding values of life. When a proper mix of work, recreation, and exercise has been attained, when we can savor the pleasure of self growth, and enjoy our children, then we can honestly feel that the "evil money" of Euripides is as far removed from us as the progress which separates our respective civilizations.

16) THE STREET OF DREAMS

More and more young couples are venturing into Wall Street with the hope of making their fortune there. The decision to invest is usually promoted by what now amounts to social pressure. The particular stock which they buy is recommended to them by a well meaning friend, one who may have made a profit in the stock.

The fact that a stock is touted by a friend is not wrong in itself. It should be intelligently followed up and researched. A broker should be engaged to investigate the company and its prospects. After the proper inquiries nothing is wrong with purchasing a promising stock.

Tragedy befalls many new investors as a result of their greed. They usually hasten to buy a stock before investigating it. They fear that it will go up in price while they are waiting. They learn by bitter first-hand experience that the "Street" is a boulevard... it goes both ways, up and down.

In the aftermath of the disappointment, they find more to argue about, and are quick to anger at each other. One blames the other for deciding to buy the stock. They develop a mutual distaste for their friend who raved about his profit. Suddenly, the stock market becomes the major cause of unhappiness in the household, replacing the usual mother-in-law trouble.

The unhappiness is compounded in many cases where complete savings accounts are wiped out. Unthinking persons in the heat of their greed and in their ignorance of the workings of the market invest all of their wedding gifts and hard earned savings in a speculative situation. The guilt is in their ignorance, and not in their action. They should act with suspicion, for speculation is the result of someone's tip.

This admonition does not apply only to those who have gambled and lost. It should serve as a warning and a lesson to those who are about to invest, and those who have made money in the market. If you have speculated and won, you can consider yourself lucky. The misfortunes of millions of people are legend. Let us have the mistakes of others serve our advantage. The utmost precaution and the following requirements are necessary before risking a dollar of your money. Allow a comfortable amount of savings to take care of daily necessities and any emergencies which may arise. Have a minimum of life insurance; an amount which is arrived at mutually by your insurance broker and yourself. Beyond these requirements you are ready for the stock market.

If you are interested in the market, there are many ways to learn about a stock including writing directly to the company for annual reports and other informative literature. Standard and Poor's, Fitch's, and Moody's are the three leading statistical services which are a vital source of market information.

When you have educated yourself in the ways of the "Street," and once you are able to calmly sift the information you hear and investigate it thoroughly... it will be only a matter of time until your grief, sorrow, and arguments will turn to happiness and joy. Your wise investments will result in a profitable reality on the "Street of Dreams."

17) THE SERVICES

Every Monday morning registered representatives eagerly await the recommendations of advisory services. These companies are influential in brokerage circles, and their following with the public is growing increasingly because of their aggressive policy of recruiting new members.

It is obvious to anyone who reads the business section of the Sunday New York Times that the advertising of the various service companies has assumed alarming proportions. In fact, the Federal Trade commission has warned these companies to temper their outlandish claims. Apparently, the admonition was only partially successful. The claims and predictions are as dramatic as ever. The following are just a few samples of their pulse-quickening headlines: CANDIDATES FOR STOCK SPLITS IN TODAY'S MARKETS... 118 stocks of firms that have never shown a loss or missed a dividend in 30 to 124 years. Blue chip science stocks with dynamic potentials. Stocks which are outperforming the averages!

These headlines would make one think that it was easy to win in the market. Just send in a handful of dollar bills to the advisory services and they will send you the answer to your prayers. There are several reasons why it is impossible to be one hundred percent sure that the "tip sheets" can make you a successful investor. Even the experts who edit and compile the favorite lists of the advisory services would have to reluctantly admit to the following: Not one service can claim a record of complete success in its predictions. Investors can hardly afford to buy all the stocks which are recommended. Therefore, it is still up to the subscriber to select a stock. This selection may or may not perform as expected. Some investors have scored well with certain services and they avidly recommend them to their friends and business acquaintances. Others switch from one service to another without any luck.

In today's selective market, it has become very important to buy intelligently. The bear and the bull are living together. Even those who use a service and buy its favorite stocks should not accept a reversal with amazement. Decisions are made by human beings. They make mistakes until they can no longer make decisions. Take your loss with a ton of salt... try another situation. Remember, demand makes the price of a stock go up, and if stock buyers like the name of a company called Xerox, they will bid it up to two hundred times earnings. At the same time, a solid earner and dividend payer called Anaconda will be selling at eight times earnings, and no one will be in a hurry to buy it.

This human element in the market is the unknown quantity which both upsets and delights various people. Obviously, the ones who lose are upset, and the ones who are riding a winner are delighted. How can tangible and sensible realities predict the course of a shadowy and chameleon-like entity. This is the hidden roadblock to high average stock forecasting. The advisory services, with all their brains and research, cannot be so sure of their predictions. The romance stock of today is tomorrow's wall-flower.

We're all in it for the glory... the glory of the money, that is. We can't allow others to do the thinking for us, even if they do the picking. A stock market trader must weigh the composite opinion of broker, service, and friends. Then he must make his own decision. Shortly thereafter, other decisions must be made... whether to sell if the stock goes down or if it goes up. The screaming headlines of the services have little bearing on the crucial decisions which the stockholder himself must make. On these alone will his success or failure in the market depend.

18) LOSING HURTS BAD

Sadness, frustration, and fear deepen the lines in the face of a person threatened with a loss in the stock market. The stark reality of a shrinking capital, drains the optimism and chills the blood of even the most callous investor. It is hard for one who has not had the experience to imagine what a magnetic grasp a falling stock can have on a person. The specter of the loss pervades his entire existence, and the irretrievable reality saps his enthusiasm and vitality.

This unenviable position of a loser in the stock market is not an unusual one. Many people have suffered more losses than profits, and undoubtedly many others will do the same.

The temptation of a killing is greater than the pain of a suspected loss. This works only in theory. The aggravation and complications caused by a loss of money through speculation can really be equated with the delight at making a profit. The extremes of happiness and dejection are the two end products of stock speculation. They are as far apart as the poles, but paradoxically are equal in emotional intensity. Let us experience along with the customer the thrills of a speculative winner, and the disaster of a loss.

Mr. Y is a man of modest means. A customer of his urges him to buy Motor Products which is traded on the New York Stock Exchange. It is trading at about sixteen. The person who does the recommending is a garrulous type and is usually prone to exaggeration. Because of his personality, Mr. Y is justifiably doubtful. However, with the constant prodding of his talkative friend, and the advice of a broker, our Mr. Y finally buys 100 shares of Motor Products at 18 dollars a share. The price had advanced two dollars a share while our Mr. Y was deciding.

Almost immediately after he buys the stock it starts to trade violently and go up three, six, and even eleven dollars a day! The demand for the stock was prompted by good earnings and the possibility of several acquisitions. The reason for the wild gyrations in the stock was that the capitalization was small. That means that there were only a small number of shares outstanding. When an issue is "thin" in the jargon of the street, any sort of demand can send a stock rocketing all the way up. This is what happened to Motor Products. In one month the stock rose to a high of sixty dollars a share.

What was happening to Mr. Y while the stock was morfe than tripling? Well, he was in the throes of a passionate trance. His step was lively, he smiled almost all the time, and he abounded in happiness and the milk of human kindness. His wife shared his joy and translated her pride in him with acts uncommonly rare. All was serene, as it usually is with a winner. It doesn't matter whether or not Mr. Y sells his stock, the profit is there, and is his for the taking.

Mr. X is an ambitious young man who has heard so much about the money that has been made in the stock market that he is willing to gamble most of his hard earned life savings to try his luck. The way his friends brag about their investments it almost sounds like a sure thing. One of Mr. X's closest friends made thousands of dollars in Texas Instruments. This company is no fly-by-night speculation.. It is perhaps the largest firm in the Electronics Industry. Despite these facts 250 dollars a share seems to be quite expensive for any stock, no matter how good. Nr. X asks a broker's advice, and he is assured that Texas Instruments is one of the best growth stocks, and the electronics Industry promises to have a new spurt of growth in the 1960s due to the expanded efforts of our country in space.

With confidence and hope that is reinforced by his friend and broker, our stockholder invests almost all of his savings. He buys 50 shares of Texas Instruments at

254 dollars a share. The day of his purchase the stock goes up to 257 dollars a share. Mr. X cannot contain his elation. He is almost sorry that he didn't buy more than 50 shares. Even though he bought the stock for long term growth, he enjoyed seeing a profit on the first day. The joy was short lived. Soon Texas Instruments started to dip. It moved steadily downward. When the price stood at 231 our disquieted Mr. X was numb with fear. His friend and broker could not rationally explain why the stock went down. They argued that there was nothing to worry about. After all, this was Texas Instruments, and it was bought for the long term anyway. It would turn around. A twenty-four point loss meant a deficit of twelve hundred dollars if he sold. Mr. X was too paralyzed to take any action, besides he was hopeful that the stock would reverse itself. Several weeks went by during which our friend spent sleepless nights. He looked for news items to bolster his faltering optimism.

Unfortunately there were no longer encouraging predictions for the Electronics Industry. Instead, researchers were talking about "the coming shakeout in the Electronics Industry." There was no fear for the future of Texas Instruments, but rising costs and price cutting to meet competition were reducing profit margins. These were certainly not the ingredients for growth. By this time, the stock was 200 dollars a share, a twenty-five hundred dollar paper loss. How could he take such a beating? Fear had changed to panic. Mr. X was living a bad dream. His work was affected by his mental attitude. His wife was so angry that she continually nagged him about his mistake. His friend who was also suffering with the stock's slide rarely tried to commiserate with him. He was having his own troubles. The broker could find no words of solace either.

One day, Texas Instruments released a poor earnings report for the first half of 1961. The end of the world had come for our Mr. X, or so he thought. The stock responded to the bad news with a quip drop to 175. What could he do? He had done a terrible thing. Ten years of hard earned savings going down the drain because of his greed! But still Mr. X was too scared to sell.

Things did not improve with Texas Instruments, and the price of the stock kept going down. What made things more aggravating was that many other stocks in the market were going up, and the Dow Jones Averages were setting new highs. The romance and glamour had gone out of the Electronics Industry, and so did the color in Mr. X's face. He was a pale, lifeless, and emotionally drained individual. He sat by and watched his stock plummet through 130 and go down as low as 123 dollars a share. Life had no more joy. He was just going through the motions. It seemed as if nothing mattered except this one big problem, which he had to face alone.

By some unknown force of desperation our beleaguered Mr. X was able to get up enough courage to call his broker and put in an order to sell. He finally got out at 128 dollars a share. He had taken a loss of $6,300 dollars. His dreams of riches were shattered. He was a sadder but wiser man. The cancer which was plaguing his very existence had been extirpated. There was some feeling of relief, but the scars remained, and would be a memory and lesson for life.

It was small consolation for Mr. X that Texas Instruments continued to fall until it hit 50 dollars a share. It was almost unimaginable to him that he could have lost more than he did. It is now easy to see that his suffering would have continued for quite a while longer, not only while TXN was dipping to 50 , but also when the new surge of interest in the electronics stocks developed, with the development of integrated circuits, cause Texas instruments to once again lead the industry back to the heights it had once known.

Every day there are thousands of Mr. Y's and Mr. X's entering the market. The two sides of the market you have just seen through their examples should serve as a moral. The vagaries of a fickle market should be fully understood by all who tempt fate. It is no playground for graduates of "Monopoly." This game is played with real money, and losing it hurts, and hurts bad.

19) THE BIG SHOT

They met on a subway station at eight o'clock in the morning.

" I want to be a big shot!" the disheveled man said unashamedly. His friend raised an eyebrow as he carefully scrutinized his clothing.

"I bought a thousand shares of this stock at 25 cents a share... if it goes up to 50 cents I'm doubling my money!"

He stood there with an old double breasted navy jacket which had already turned purple.

"I can't buy A.T.&T. or IBM.. who can afford such high prices? How much can I buy..two shares.. three shares? Besides, I'm a gambler... I want to make a fast buck!"

His shoes were brown underneath the dirt, and his tie did not match the brightly colored argyle socks.

"I like to buy round lots," he went on. $ 2 dollars, $ 3 dollars, that way I can buy two or three hundred shares of a stock and I feel I got something!"

His tie represented a scene from the Peloponnesian

War. There was a trireme in gold set against a maroon background. It was hand painted.

"You see it's like this," he explained. "I bought a stock last year at seven dollars a share. The name was Bellanca. I fell asleep while it went all the way down to a quarter. I gave it up for lost. All of a sudden, out of a clear blue sky, it started to move. It went all the way back to four dollars a share. So I sold it and switched into consolidated Sun Ray at 1 ½ dollars a share. So what did it cost me? I never figured to get anything from Bellanca. I'm playing with their money!"

His shirt was brown. The top button was missing so he compensated for it by making a huge Windsor knot which was lost in the valley of his extra long pointed collar.

"How's the family?" queried his anxious friend.

"The same, thank you," parried our big Stock Market operator.

"Say," said his friend, "I hate to bring this up. It seems so trivial after all this conversation about big money, but when are you going to pay me back the five bucks you owe me?"

Just then the train rumbled in, and over the noise of

the jostling crowd, barely audible, came this reply.

"Have a heart," he said, "I only borrowed it last week!"

20) THE STOCK DOCTOR

Too many people have the mistaken notion that a doctor has a magic wand that can make them rich. In the same way the public looks to a doctor for that supernatural gift of curing the sick, it endows the registered representative with a special formula for achieving monetary gain. No one has a sure fire method of winning in Wall Street... if he did he wouldn't tell anyone about it... he would keep it to himself.

A broker is essentially a salesman, and as is true in the case of most salesmen, he must first sell himself to his customer. Once he has built up a certain amount of rapport and confidence, he can go about his business of suggesting, researching, and recommending stocks. He is not possessed of any superhuman power or knowledge of the future. The stock market has many disillusioned people who thought they knew it all.

A doctor acts in the following manner; he checks his patient's symptoms, discusses his case, gives his prognosis, and finally prescribes medication to purge the disease and alleviate the pain or discomfort. A broker proceeds in a similar way. He has a certain stock to appraise. He checks its past history, its present financial condition, and with a careful study of the facts he can make an intelligent prediction about the future of the company. The stock doctor, which a broker really is, lacks only one thing... he has no medicine to prescribe if the stock starts to go down. His only prescription can be to sell.

There many other factors which tug at the direction of a stock, but as a rule a company with a sound record of growth will usually continue to grow, and at much the same pace.

Let us then come to an understanding about the manner in which we come to the bar of decision. Your broker is informed, he is sympathetic to your wishes, and he is anxious in most cases for you to buy. His knowledge does not extend into the arms of the supernatural. He will be glad to help you with information about any company, but when it comes to the crucial decision, you will be quite alone with the responsibility.

Do not fear these decisions... they are not irrevocable. If you find that you have made the wrong choice you can always sell at a small loss and retain your principle. Do not quail or quiver in the valley of decision. Remember that the mountain nearby is densely populated with well-wishing friends and your broker, who are rooting for you to pick a winner.

21) PRIDE OF OWNERSHIP

One of the most heart-warming benefits of investing in the stock market is the feeling of belonging. Pride of ownership can make a little man (in the financial sense) feel big. A stockholder with one share of American Telephone commands the same attention as did the late Billy Rose. He has voting privileges, he receives the same correspondence, and he is entitled to attend the annual meeting.

American industry, the colossus of world capitalism is a cold, unfeeling mass of figures. The competition which pits industry against industry, and company against company allows little time for sentiment or other human sensitivities. It is only when one becomes identified with a particular corporation that the spirit, the chauvinism, and the "esprit de corps" begins to take hold.

Those who buy stock for speculative purposes are not apt to be affected by this affinity for as company. They can't afford to develop a feeling of belonging because it would make it difficult to sell the stock. A trader's credo is always "don't fall in love with a stock."

Investors with long range programs find it

psychologically advantageous to enjoy their ownership of a corporation's stock. When it is possible they buy products which the company makes. For years they receive news of the company's progress. They also attend the annual meetings when it is convenient to meet with the officers. All of these things instill in a stockholder an almost religious fervor for the company of their selection. This fervor varies directly with the amount of profit which resides in the price of the shares. There are few cases on record of shareholders who proudly boast of owning a stock in a company which is not doing well.

There are hundreds of companies which have achieved a high level of prestige with investors throughout the years. They have gained their status by dint of their consistent growth and good dividend records. They have demonstrated such a superiority in their respective fields that their corporate image gives status to their stockholders. A few companies which stand out in this sense are the following: IBM, Exxon, DuPont, General Electric, American Telephone and Merck and Co.

One should not feel offended if he does not own any of the companies mentioned. There are many fine, outstanding, progressive, and worthwhile companies which stockholders are proud to own. Management companies of investment trusts have shown their confidence in the companies mentioned by consistently buying their stock. This is a vote of confidence in these corporations, and should be a source of pride to investors all over the world who own their stock.

22) COMPANY MOTTOS

Growth, excellence, quality, research, progress, and integrity are some of the bywords of companies which help build their corporate image. It is of the utmost importance for companies who make consumer products to instill in the public an unshakeable confidence, and the best way to accomplish is to make a superior product. In addition to that it is also advisable to build a feeling of loyalty in the hearts and minds of employees who help manufacture those quality products. The best way to achieve that is to develop a company motto which stirs the imagination and moves the spirit.

"The Magnificent Magnavox," "Better Things For Better Living Through Chemistry," You Can Be Sure If it's Westinghouse," Where Research Is The Key To Tomorrow," "The Most Trusted name In Electronics," "A Hand In things To come." These are just a few of the mottos which have become a part of industrial advertising. They convey an image of stability, reliability, and excellence in the mind of the consumer, and directly help to sell the products and build sales. The late Thomas Watson Se. of great IBM built one of the largest and soundest industrial complexes in the world, and his helper was a watchword in all of IBM's plants and offices throughout the world... it is simply the word THINK.

It would be far-fetched to suppose that the group of words or phrases used to describe a feeling or idea of quality and superiority in the mind of the public can be the sole ingredient in the recipe for success in a company. Everyone knows that sound management, prudent economy, foresight in planning, and excellence of product are the elements which combine in earning the desired reputation. Once this allegiance has been built up through years of consistency, it is an alert public relations department which capitalizes on the established record for quality. A catchword or phrase which will bring the company's name to mind, or better still a motto which mentions the company's name will do two things; it will make faithful customers proud of their loyalty, and will bring thousands of others flocking to their banner. What is more, employees will work with a new feeling of belonging. They will carry their pride like a badge of honor, and happily spread the contagion to their friends and neighbors.

23) THE IBM SAGA

"My wife never was interested in the stock market until I bought IBM," said Bennie animatedly. His voice was quivering with intensity as he continued to explain.

"I've had a lot of good stocks, Zenith, Crown cork, General electric, and others, but nothing excited her more than owning IBM," he continued with feeling.

"She has what amounts to a religious attachment to this stock, and you can't blame her," he said with a smile.

I was caught up in the pessimism which was generated by the plummeting electronics stocks. Texas Instruments, Avnet, Standard Kollsman, and Transitron, had all been going down steadily without any noticeable support. My profit after two years of accumulating IBM one share at a time was close to four thousand dollars. I had already taken a $5,300 dollar loss this year and a profit would not cost me any tax. I planned to take a profit in IBM and then buying it back immediately. This is permissible when you are taking a profit. When you are selling to establish a loss, what is called a "wash sale," you must wait thirty days before you may buy the stock.

I was becoming wary of the stock because of the electronics' decline, and I was watching it closely. Finally, I decided to play it safe and place a sell-stop order. The stock was selling at $565. I set the order at $525...a leeway of twenty dollars a share. Three days later I was sold out, and on the day of the sale the price sank to $517. I felt very good about taking the profit and having the opportunity to buy the stock back at a lower price. The opportunity was no longer available because the next day IBM opened at $525 up eight dollars, and closed ten dollars higher on the day at $527. This happened in a bad market... proof of IBM's insulation against the frailties of the general market.

I was still two points off my selling price, so I didn't worry... tomorrow is another day, I thought. And I was right. The next day IBM opened at $535, up eight and closed strong at $540, up thirteen dollars on the day. It was lunch hour of that day when Ben buttonholed me.

We were friends for a couple of years, and shared the mutual joy of owning IBM. The amazing coincidence was that Ben had sold his stock the same day that I did, and for the same reason... to take the profit. The difference was that he astutely bought his stock back at the opening the following morning. He had to pay a premium for the stock, but it didn't run away from him as it was doing with me.

When he saw me a sad, almost mournful expression darkened his visage. He motioned to me to take a seat beside him, and here is where we pick up our story.

"I want you to know that no company in the market is so independent of the news. A major portion of its sales comes from rentals. If they didn't take another order they'd have enough business for the next five years," he rattled on with intensity.

I sat there mutely, watching the ticker tape flash by. I nodded in agreement, because honestly I felt the way he did about IBM. He didn't have to sell me. I was sold on the stock. He was bolstering his own belief and confidence once he had almost all his money invested in that company. As he talked the tape gave fresh evidence of his sagacity. Each trade was an uptick, and his eyes brightened happily.

"You had a happy marriage," he continued, "don't leave someone who loves you," he philosophized.

"I don't intend to," I answered. "I am just as confident about IBM's future as you are. 628 million dollars worth of stock is owned by this country's investment companies. If it is the favorite stock with them, who am I to argue with professionals"

"Look my friend," Bennie whined, "I don't stand to gain anything... the few shares you're going to buy won't make the price go up. I just don't feel right seeing you without that stock."

The sincerity that oozed from his conversation , and that poured from his lips were more than convincing. I didn't need any prompting to like IBM. I wasn't one of those "It's too high" or the "how many shares can I buy" types. I was definitely planning to buy the stock. I just happened to outsmart myself. I became too cute for my own good. I would sell for the profit, and then buy the stock back at a lower price and make a few hundred dollars more on the new purchase. Only it didn't work that way. The stock moved twenty-three points in two days, and here I was with a sixteen point gap to bridge, licking my wounds.

The hurt wasn't so much the few hundred dollars that it would cost to replace the stock. It was a matter of pride. All the vaunted principles which I held dear were shattered by instant fears, unchecked whispers, and emotional market fever. That I could have allowed anything to upset my plan of growth for my children's education was praying heavily on my conscience. Objectively, I couldn't be unhappy because I had a healthy profit... everybody knows that they don't come easy.

There is a moral hidden somewhere in this experience. Regardless of which growth stock you may own, stand by your convictions... don't let rumors or the opinions of others make you stray from your planned program. Decisions are hard enough to make... when they are made don't alter them. Don't cause new problems by creating the need for new decisions.

My friend Ben's imploring had already made its point My mind was made up and I rallied into action. In less time than it takes to change one's mind I called my broker and bought my precious IBM stock, and with it, my peace of mind.

24) WHO HAS THE RIGHT TO GAMBLE?

There is a paradox at work in the stock market which is detrimental to the average person. This living contradiction revolves around the question of who should have the right to gamble. Many people have strong opinions on that subject, and reams of copy urging caution are printed by member firms of the New York Stock Exchange every year, but speculation continues unabated.

The most flagrant example of a rampant and uncontrollable gambling spree was the rash of new underwritings in 1961. Brokers were advised by their customers to buy anything and everything they could, as long as it was a new issue. There was rarely a stock-buyer who cared about the company's record. Few people saw the prospectus which is the legal necessity in buying any new issue. The envy which warmed the public caused a blind, wild plunge into the unknown. The remarkable thing about that era was that most people were able to make money quickly. That was tragic because when it ended, there were many who were holding the bag. The over-the-counter market was boiling pretty good in the spring of 1967 and it would not take much to cause a recurrence of the bust of 1962. New issues are once again coming out at a premium, although there are not as many as in 1961.

It is a fact which is borne out by statistics that the average new investor is a man or woman of modest means. This very fact, along with sound, intelligent reasoning should dictate that speculation of any kind be avoided. A person with limited capital should look for the type of investments that offer growth, income, and safety. The latter should have priority over everything. The most dangerous thing to do is to "shoot dice," as the saying goes in the market. That expression refers to unsound, unwise, and foolish speculation. The principles of intelligent investing sounds nice on paper, but unfortunately there are many reasons why they are rarely practiced.

The urge to make money is the spur which causes new people to enter the stock market. This urge, which is natural, is set aflame by get-rich-quick stories of friends, glowing research reports of brokerage houses, and tempting, hair-raising headlines of advisory services. In view of the barrage of literature to which a tyro investor is subjected, it is not surprising that he chooses the fastest way to make a dollar... speculation. The fact that it is also the quickest way to lose a dollar is rarely of consequence until it is too late.

Poor people have no right to be in the stock market. The money they make is needed for groceries and rent. The person with a little savings can't afford to throw his money away recklessly. It should be invested wisely according to a well thought out plan. The registered representative is happy to buy and sell stock because the commission is his livelihood. He would be wrong to talk you out of a speculative purchase for fear that it may work out. In many cases his cautionary remarks are not enough to overcome your fresh enthusiasm for a speculative situation.

The well-to-do investor, on the other hand, is able to afford the advice of an investment counselor. His assets are professionally managed on a continuing basis, and he can take a flyer in a speculative situation if he feels like it. He can also stand the loss of a few thousand dollars if it is necessary. He is not happy about losing the money, nobody is, but it doesn't cause him a loss of sleep.

So we see that those who can't afford risks are always taking them. Those who can well afford to speculate, do so without the compelling needs of the former.

The onslaught will continue unhampered by the controlling influence of reason. Market volume depends on speculation, and the commercially-minded services will capitalize on human greed and fear. Brokers will buy and sell as their accounts build to the crest of excitement. The speculative fever will kill off some, and it will harden others through experience. Those of modest means who are lucky enough to survive might ultimately join the magic millions who speculate for fun.

25) EVERYTHING GOES DOWN

A mass feeling of persecution has gripped the tenants of Wall Street. They claim that whenever they buy a stock it invariably goes down. This plague affects everybody, it seems, and a simple solution would be to sell a stock short... but then the reverse would happen... the stock would go up... and the predicament would be the same.

It is absurd to believe that all stocks are constantly going down or up, but there are many unfortunate people who have experienced an immediate drop in the price of their stocks. Let us examine what actually happens to a trio of careful investors who risk their money only after thorough research and on the best advice obtainable.

Stockholder A has been told by his broker that DCA (Dynamics Corporation of America) is headed for great things. To prove his point to A, several research reports and recommendations are produced. At the time of the tip DCA is selling at 14 dollars a share. While stockholder A is asking around and reading the reports, and perhaps waiting for his wife to approve, Dynamics Corporation stock is starting to move to twenty. As it gradually moves up Mr. A begins to believe his broker and the research recommendations. When he finally becomes convinced that h should buy the stock it is selling at 21 dollars a share. He places an order and finally acquires the stock at 21 ½. The stock reaches a buying climax at 22 before an excellent piece of news is released by the company. It is announced that business is booming, and many new defense orders are expected. This news was undoubtedly the driving force behind the extended rise. As soon as the news is out the stock starts to decline. All the investors who picked the stock up earlier are selling to take their profit.

Mr. A who has finally become convinced that he has a winner will not admit to himself that he has waited too long. He interprets the good news released by the company as a bullish sign, despite the fact that the price keeps going down. When the stock reacts to generally bad business and international news by continuing its gradual decline, Mr. a finally becomes worried. At 12 ¾ our sorry friend swallows his bitter pill and takes his loss. What did he do that was wrong? He bought too high and sold too low? Don't be funny. His timing was bad. He waited too long to act on good information. Better luck next time.

Investor B has heard of all the good fortune that his friends have had with new issues. It really is not a matter of what to buy, it is a question of who you know, and how much stock he can get for you. A new underwriting was being planned by an electronic company called "Milo Electronics." What could be better than an electronics stock? Still Mr. B was cautious by nature and wanted to know more about the company. While he was trying to find out, the stock started trading on the American Stock Exchange and became one of the many spectacular new successes. It traded heavily up through 13, 14, 15, 16, etc. By the time it was selling at 18 dollars a share Mr. B was frantic, and he placed an order to buy Milo at the market before he missed the boat entirely. The following morning Milo electronics sold as high as 19 and 3/8. Our friend was lucky to get his 200 shares at 19. At this time Mr. B was no longer concerned with what the company did; he was just interested in making money. The fact is that Milo electronics is a distributor of electronic parts, TV tubes, etc. When the novelty of the new symbol MLO wore off, Milo started to fall. The fact that it was a new issue couldn't keep it from an inevitable decline. Demand dried up and anxious speculators were looking to take their profits and run. Down and down went the price, as Mr. B suffered interminably. Finally, at 13 ¼, our unlucky friend bailed himself out with a loss of $1,200 dollars. The whole cycle took only three or four weeks, but it had a more lasting effect on our Mr. B.

C was a prudent young man with a head on his shoulders. No speculation for him, he couldn't be tempted with garbage... only the best stocks for him. With this guiding principle, and with the blessings of his broker, Mr. C bought 100 shares of MMM (Minnesota Mining & Manufacturing Co.) at 86 ½ dollars a share. There is no doubt about the quality of the company, or the history of its growth. Its soundness is a matter of solid fact established through years of living proof. Despite this thoroughgoing excellence Minnesota Mining was definitely in a period of lull. Its price dropped with aggravating consistency for a period of six months until it settled in the low 70s. Now this may be a good golf score, but for Mr. C it represented a paper loss in the neighborhood of $1,400... and no sane person likes that kind of neighborhood. True... if Mr. C has patience and can ride out the dips, he will eventually live to see a profit in MMM. However, it is difficult for any person to accept with equanimity a reversal of this magnitude, and with our Mr. C the grain of salt serves only to season the egg.

The mistake which is common to all three men is a lack of timing. A and B made the further mistake of being loyal to a speculative stock on the way down. If such a situation doesn't work out immediately, it is foolish to sit by and watch your loss build up. Sell soon and lose less. In C's case, the fear will change to delight in time. MMM's doesn't stay behind for long.

In sum, let us clearly understand that it is not at all true every time somebody buys a stock that a stock goes down, nor is the reverse true... that a stock always goes up. There is rather a strong balance between the two. Our investors must realize that wishing will not make it so, as the song says. If you pick a loser, don't stay with it too long. If you have a winner, secure your profit by setting a floor on its backward movement. If you've bought a growth stock for a long term gain, buy more when lower prices afford you the opportunity. The rules are clear... subdue the emotion as much as possible, and forge a mature, intelligent approach to market mechanics. With these advantages you will never have to fall back on the stale excuse that everything you buy inevitably goes down.

26) ODD LOTS

According to reliable statistics, odd-lot trading today represents close to ten percent of the total trading on the listed stock exchanges. This is no mean amount of business, or an easy job to handle. It takes the full time employment of hundreds of people by the two odd-lot dealers, DeCoppet and Doremus and Carlisle and Jacqueline.

The odd-lot public is that much maligned group which is always supposed to be wrong. Of course, every now and then you read about some person who is found amid the comfort of a large cache, which almost always includes enough stock certificates to stuff an oversized mattress. Usually this stock started out as ten share lots and through the years the many stock dividends and splits grew into the fortune which was discovered. This odd-lot investor certainly could not have been wrong.

Millions of new investors who will soon join the ranks will feel their way in the market by means of the odd-lots. Many of the uninitiated do not realize that it is possible to buy stock in small amounts which cost very little in dollars and cents. They still have the mistaken impression that it takes thousands of dollars to be a stockholder.

There is only one disadvantage in buying or selling odd-lots and that is the premium which must be paid. On the New York Stock Exchange when you buy a stock under fifty-five dollars a share, there is a charge of one eighth of a point or twelve and one half cents a share. If the stock is over fifty-five you pay a quarter or twenty-five cents. When you sell an odd-lot the same premium must be paid. This is the price that the odd-lot dealers charge for the performance of their intricate task retailing the round lots and breaking them down to your particular size..

On the American Stock Exchange the specialists handle the odd-lots in their stocks, and charge a fee of one eighth under forty and one quarter over forty. All odd-lots over-the-counter are free of since there is no record of the exact time of the trade upon which to base the effective sale. This effective sale is the price of the first round lot after your odd-lot order reaches the floor of the exchange. Each order is time-stamped when it reaches the odd-lot dealer so that you can check the validity of the price with the tape sales. They are also timed accurately to serve as a record for the current pricing of all odd-lots. I should have stated at the outset that an odd-lot is usually less than one hundred shares.

A round lot is usually one hundred shares or more.

It should be fairly obvious that it is within the reach of even the most financially humble to own the greatest names of corporate America. The happy feeling of ownership and possession is just as real for a person who owns two shares of a stock as it is for a mogul with ten thousand. In most cases the feeling is stronger in the man with the lesser amount of shares, for it may represent a larger percentage of his total worth.

Unlike the ownership of a mutual fund whose ownership includes a proportionate interest in a widely diversified portfolio, concentrated ownership of several corporations allows one to identify with the company and its products.

It has recently become socially acceptable to give and receive as gifts, prizes, and rewards, small amounts of common stocks. A greater number of corporations are adding employee stock option plans to induce loyalty and decrease turnover.

The net effect of this growing popularity of stock giving has been to swell the tide of ownership, and by means of the odd-lot, open the eyes of thousands to the excitement and fascination that is Wall Street.

27) PRICE TIMES EARNINGS

A company whose sales and earnings have shown a consistent increase over a period of several years usually commands an above average premium of price over its earnings. This comparison is known as price times earnings ratio (p/e ratio), or "the multiple." In the past this ratio was a tool of analysts in their evaluation of a company. Today the average investor considers it important when deciding whether or not to buy a stock.

Of course, a company with expanding profit margins in an explosive phase of its earnings growth can shrink its price earnings ratio at a very rapid pace. Therefore, the price of the stock may discount these earnings for one or more years in advance. Recent examples of this phenomenon are Xerox, Polaroid, Itek, E.G.&G. and Solitron Devices. In almost all of these situations a high short position causes an excessive demand and results in sharply rising prices. Let us examine one of the companies in detail.

In 1966, Solitron Devices had a high of 173 and a low of 60 ½. Earnings in fiscal 1965 ending February were $1.65 adjusted for a stock split. In other words, at the high Solitron was selling at 100 times earnings. The sharp selloff during 1966 took the stock down to a point where it was selling at close to 20 times the expected three dollars in fiscal 1967. This volatile performer is now selling at 260 dollars a share in July 1967. Some estimates of earnings in the new fiscal period range from five to as much as seven or eight dollars a share. There is no one who could predict the exact earnings or the multiple which this performer will command six months or a year from this writing.

Predictions and estimates are only assumptions. Sales and earnings cannot be made to grow with precision from year to year. There is no set formula as to how high a P/E ratio a stock should deserve. It varies with the industry. Those industries with constant or erratic earnings records usually have a low ratio of about 10 or 12 times earnings. Growth stocks have rising earnings and can support ratios of from 25 to 50 times and even higher. The ratio declines in direct proportion to the rise in earnings.

Standard and Poor's has a Rapid Growth Stock list which is composed of 200 companies. By means of a computer the growth rate is figured and stocks are and deleted from the list. There is no sure thing... even in the field of growth. But all other things being equal, a company which has grown for many years will continue to grow. Management projects increases for the New

Year and can almost predict its new sales and earnings.
A faltering economy can upset these predictions, but the
management cannot be blamed for that. How
wonderful it would be if we could predict the course of a
stock's price. It might take the fun out of the market...
but it sure would add enjoyment to the rest of your life!

28) YOU CAN'T GO WRONG

It is undoubtedly true that anybody connected with the market will admit that all investment in common stock contains some element of risk. I therefore fail to see how a tranquilizing expression such as "You Can't go Wrong" can have developed such a loyal following.

Exponents of the "How far wrong can you go" school do not just make the statement blandly and let it go at that. They usually cite chapter and verse, the reasons why your investment in a particular stock will cause you no heartaches or sleepless nights.

The companies which are proposed are almost always "solid" ones. They also pay a fairly liberal dividend. They also contend that the industry of which the corporation is a part is on the threshold of a great advance, and this company's backlog of orders is bound to keep their business booming.

Experience has shown with painful clarity just how wrong some of these investments can be. In quick succession a dividend can be cut, a contract can be cancelled, and a whole industry can be depressed. The result is often a protracted decline in the price of the stock... a stock in which "You couldn't go wrong!"

There are many safeguards which can be used to avoid the lapse into a tranquil submission or error. The first step is to accept advice with caution... not disdain. Many good tips are often lost because we are cautious to an extreme. Listen to everything... but do not believe anything until solid digging proves it out. There is time enough to get on a good thing once you've proven to yourself there is a bona fide potential in its future.

Do not mock the beliefs or feelings of any of your friends and acquaintances. They are sincere in their convictions, and don't mean you any harm. In fact, they believe they are doing you a favor.

Secondly, and this is important in any investment, keep in constant touch with the price of your stock. If you are too busy to do it yourself, tell your broker to keep you informed daily. If a stock is purchased through recommendation and it does not perform as promised, sell it. We can't expect everything to work out profitably the least we can do is to limit the loss.

Thirdly, and most important, have the intelligence and maturity to reject anything you've overheard in an elevator, subway train, or a restaurant. Check the source of your information. The news itself is not as important as the person who disseminates it. Make sure you also clear the information with your broker before you make a firm decision to buy.

Finally, in the clear light of reason, you will have ended all doubts about the accuracy of this tip. Your mind will be at ease... the deep, dark secret, the aura of mystery about the stock will be uncovered. You can then dive headlong into the situation with the positive, informed, and reassuring knowledge that "You can't go wrong!"...or can you?

29) LOCKED IN

The colorful jargon of Wall Street has no axiom which compares in imagery with the phrase "Locked In." the uninitiated might think that it had something to do with jail or incarceration! The fact is that the person who experiences this locked in position is really free in the physical sense; it is only his mind that wears the chains.

The most common sense of this situation is neglect on the part of the stockholder. That persists and an underlying optimism which paradoxically flourishes in adversity. The reason for this stubborn hope is unfounded. After all, can a watermelon grow in the desert and be nourished by its sandy wastes?

Every investor who buys a stock does so with the expectation of a profit. The trouble is that enthusiasm dies too slowly, and his reluctance to sell quickly when a stock goes the wrong way inevitably leads to trouble. The gradual erosion of a stock's price, and the utter paralysis and inaction of the stockholder lead to a Nirvana... a world where the sun doesn't shine, people don't smile, and stocks don't move.

This is the dismal abyss of the locked in millions. They tramp unhappily into the boardrooms every day to watch the ticker tape compound their sorrow. Lethargy is their only look...inertia their restraining yoke. If reason can disperse the gloom, they may finally sell their troublemakers. When this happens they gain a twofold freedom. They free themselves of the agony of owning a sick stock, and they free the balance of their funds from further deterioration.

Let us now examine another group of unhappy investors in the stock market. Theirs is not an agony of despair like their losing counterpart. These people are locked in on the upside. Their cups are running over. I shed no tears for them just because someone wants to take the egg out of their beer. These stockholders refuse to sell only because the profits they make will have to be shared with the Treasury Department. Their prison is a much more bearable one.

The Income Tax code states that unless a security has been held for at least one year, all profits of a stock transaction shall be deemed regular income, and taxed in the normal bracket of the investor. It is only after one year that profits can be considered a long term capital gain, and then the profit is taxable at a maximum rate of twenty-eight percent.

It is therefore quite understandable for a fortunate winner who is locked in on the upside to be perturbed. There are many people who have immense profits in growth stocks such as Apple, Netflix, Amazon, Boeing,, Priceline, and others. They are even reluctant to take a long term capital gain because they have to pay so much money to the government. Their only chance of getting hurt is the unlikely possibility of a downward movement in their stocks. If that happened their problem would be neutralized. They would no longer have such a large profit to share with the Internal Revenue.

So we see that it is possible to be "Locked In" with a loss or a profit. It should be unmistakably clear that from an objective point of view both problems can be resolved. The loser must swallow hard, bury his pride, and take his loss. The winner should either hold or take his profit... but pray that he can always be Uncle Sam's partner with his winnings. They both should realize that nothing locks them in but their own hesitation and greed.

30) NOTHING WILL GET YOU NOTHING

There is a lot of free advice floating around the stock market today, and many times this advice only proves that you get what you pay for. King Lear, in Shakespeare's famous tragedy summed it up clearly when he told his daughter Cordelia, "Nothing will get you Nothing."

It is extremely difficult to face an emotional problem and arrive at a calm, rational, and successful solution. That is just what one is up against when he tries to select a stock for a possible capital gain. It is true that statistics exist for every company, and research can prove the technical worth of a given situation. Unfortunately, however, there is no proven way to isolate the sentiment of the public. This is crucial in determining the direction of the market, a particular industry, or any one issue.

If sentiment is unpredictable, then a large segment of shareowners are foolishly experiencing the mental anguish of prolonged ownership of depressed stocks. There is no sense in holding a stock, no matter how good its current or future prospects are. If the market is depressed and the price goes down consistently it isn't worth holding. It isn't even worth holding if the price stays the same! This situation gave birth to the adage, "stocks are made to sell." When you sell a poorly acting stock, you release the funds for the acquisition of a better one. There are always a handful of favorites, even in a depressed market.

The essence of this philosophy can be aptly summarized by comparing the buying of stocks to a card game. Let us say you are playing poker. Each stock you buy can be considered a new hand. I know that when I play closed poker and I have a bad hand, I'm out. I throw my cards in and look for a better hand in the next deal. I'm not angry, sore, or sorry about my loss. There's always the next game, and I have a new chance to win each time.

This can be a guide to you in the selection and handling of stocks. If the stock you buy turns out to be a loser, .sell it and look for a better one. You can't lose too much if you act quickly, and you avoid collecting a tired list of inactive stocks with paper losses.

I dully realize that one cannot be flippant and carefree in his handling of stocks as he is in a penny ante poker game. When the stocks are high the pulse beats faster. Many people say that the theory behind a quick disposal of bad stocks is all right in theory, but it doesn't work in fact. The trouble is that most stockholders are mired in the muck of their own indecision.

There is no alternative to crisp, efficient, or business-like action whether it is on your job or in the buying and selling of stocks. Suit the thought to the deed. Act promptly to protect yourself...or no one in the world will be able to help you. When you lose you are alone with your grief. Be a winner and enjoy the company of your friends, neighbors, and family.

Gaylord Mitty was sure he could win at the card table because he was a card shark. But even he did not win every deal! Let that serve as a warning to those who must sink or swim with every stock they buy. The payoff is at the bottom line, when all the chips are counted. Ride the winners all the way...but get rid of your dogs early.

31) DIVERSIFICATION AND CONCENTRATION

Among the many theories of investing in the stock market, none have had a longer or more interesting history of conflict than the broad and opposite concepts of diversification and concentration.

St the outset let us define each term so that we can know precisely what they mean and how they differ in the strict sense. The dictionary states the following: Diversify- to distribute investments among many different kinds of securities Concentrate--- to increase in strength by removing diluting material.

The proponents of the school of diversification are almost certain to use their favorite and hackneyed expression, "Don't put all your eggs in one basket," and those who concentrate usually do so in order to make a "Killing." Who is right? A review of the salient features of each philosophy will help you formulate your own opinion. Each method of investing will suit the needs of different individuals. One can't foist his opinion on others simply because it caters to his circumstances. However, we do find many people adopting the ideas of others irrespective of their own financial condition.

Many diversified portfolios include bonds, preferred stocks, and utilities, so that a fixed income is assured. When a common stock portfolio is considered, it is a matter of deciding what companies and what industries to select. Among the multitude of industry groups to choose from, the following are a representative list: Chemicals, Business Machines, Food Companies, Railroads, Electronics, Space Stocks, Oils, Metals, Vending machines, Leisure Time Stocks, Life Insurance, Automobiles, and Electrical Equipment Stocks.

With the help of a competent broker or investment counselor you can arrange a portfolio which is diversified enough to give you safety and stability. Since you are looking to insulate yourself against a dramatic loss in any one of a few stocks, you are spreading or diluting your opportunity for a dynamic gain as well. The Utilities, defensive issues, and solid dividend paying stocks can hardly be expected to make fast and spectacular gains. Even if good growth stocks are included in your list that can have little more than a balancing effect on the slow and steady progress of the rock-ribbed stocks already mentioned. The safety in numbers factor does prevail, and this is the basis of the philosophy of diversification.

Now let us turn to the wheeling and dealing type of man who doesn't believe in holding a large and varied collection of diversified stocks. For him the market is a place to make profit, and he approaches the problem from a diametrically opposed point of view. He is willing to risk safety for the chance of a quick, mercury-like gain. He accomplishes this by "getting a hunch and betting a bunch."

When research turns up a situation which is compelling, our trader seizes the opportunity. He buys a large amount of a particular stock and follows it very carefully to a conclusion. If the timing of the purchase turns out to be wrong, it is already predetermined where the stock will be sold. The same is true on the plus side. At a point where profit taking seems advisable our active speculator cashes in his chips

It is important here to point out that it is not necessary to trade in small, highly speculative companies whose price is very low. There are many well established corporations whose aggressive research and development are creating new products, and are also gaining a foothold in new areas of growth. These are the situations which beckon the interest of stock market operators... here is where the profit can be made, if the signs are discovered early enough.

Diversification is not only the target of the individual,

but of many companies as well. In an attempt to achieve a vertical status, oil companies seek crude deposits, acquire refining facilities, and buy retail outlets. This is the reason for the recent rash of oil buyouts. There are many benefits which can accrue to a company when its subsidiaries or divisions complement each other in operation. Defense firms try to gain a higher percentage of profit by merging with non-defense companies that have higher profit margins. Tobacco companies have used their enormous cash resources to ward off the damaging effect of cancer and heart disease scares by adding companies in unallied fields.

There are dangers inherent in diversification for both the individual and corporate kind. The decentralization of a company can lead to management's loss of control over the various divisions. It is just as dangerous to be overdiversified as it is to be undiversified. When the reigns of a company's management are extended too far, it can lead to inefficiency and an uneconomical operation. In the same way, an investor can have a difficult time with a portfolio which is thinly spread out over too many companies.

There are companies which have the financial abilityto add new lines ro their product mix, but they refuse to diversify. The management believes that "a shoemaker should stick to his last." It feels that a company should do what it knows best. There is sound judgment in that axiom, but it will not stop mergers and acquisitions, especially when a deal can be worked out for the benefit of all concerned.

As for the harried investor, he can buy diversification with one purchase, if he happens to pick a company which is well diversified. He can also concentrate, even while he is buying ten different stocks. They can all be in one industry. There are times when the stocks of many companies within a particular industry will move in concert. This may be the result of a new surge of business, price increases for their products, or just a revival of investor interest for that segment of the market.

Knowing the whys and wherefores of buying stock doesn't license a person with a few hundred dollars to either diversify or concentrate. He may buy stock on the Monthly Investment Plan for as little as forty dollars a quarter, or he can purchase a mutual fund for about the same amount. For this person the discussion here does not apply.

Those who are in a position to invest or speculate with substantial funds are constantly formulating new courses of action. In an active market it is important to buy the popular favorites. When the market is dull, it is best to convert your stocks into a cash reserve.

Most people in the stock market are told that they must play it safe and diversify their holdings. It makes good sense to be careful. I don't contest the intelligence of spreading the risk, or doubt the wisdom of being a well diversified, solidly entrenched, and safely invested person. I do wonder, however, how many millions of those people wistfully, and jealously eye the dynamic, magnetic, and mercurial favorites as they rocket to new highs, while their solid portfolios continue to produce a safe, steady, and unglamorous flow of dividends.

32) THE PHILOSOPHY OF BUYING

There is a mild difference of opinion among the minions of the street on the question of when is the best time to buy stocks. In the broad sense the disagreement stems from a conviction on the part of many people that the right way to buy is when a stock is way down, or as the expression goes, "bottoming out." The other school of buyers maintains that it is best to buy when a stock is on the way up. There is no clearly defined answer to this problem, and it will remain with us as long as stocks are traded. The best we can do here is to point out from the experience of others, what causes the rise and fall of stocks, and in that way we may arrive at a considered conclusion about the timing of our purchases.

There are a multitude of reasons why a stock is depressed and making new lows. The main reason is the lack of good earnings, poor sales, and the cutting or omission of dividends. The object of researchers and bargain hunters alike is to find a sleeper. This can be a quality company in a depressed state of sales and earnings. If they discover such a company early enough they have found something worthwhile. This group of people is constantly alert to the action of stocks as they make new lows every day. It is unfortunate that one cannot know the exact bottom price of a stock as it slides constantly to new lows, but that does not matter if you have really found a plum that is ripe for the picking.

The latent value of your discovery can make it climb as far as its potential will allow. If it is hit by a bad strike, for example, or it has expenses for new product development, it can slow the advance of a stock. However, the force of a company's quality, stability, and unquestioned earning power will inevitably send the price of the stock back to more respectable levels.

The other group of investors is undoubtedly a larger one. I say this in the belief that most people are attracted to a stock when it is behaving well and making new highs. In those cases it is usually better earnings and the expectation of good news in the form of a stock split or increased dividends or both which causes a stock to continue rising. Growth stocks behave this way, and it is as difficult to guess how high a stock is going to rise before "topping out," as it is to know how low it will go before "bottoming out."

The air of uncertainty which attends these problems makes the selection of stocks the inexact science it is. This compounds the wonder and fascination of the stock market. Just think how dull it would be if we knew exactly what was going to happen every time we bought a stock? The doubt about the outcome of an investment multiplies the elation when you finally do hit upon a winner. When that happens you have a new and intriguing problem... when is the right time to sell?

33) THE GAMBLING INSTINCT

The gambling instinct which is manifest in the form of speculation in the stock market is responsible to a great extent for the wonderful growth of industry. Without it the development of our natural resources would be almost impossible.

"The instinct to speculate is so strong in American men and women that they choose to take a chance regardless of the fact that at the outset they half-realize they eventually must lose."

When this loss is established the person involved is hooked forever, because as the expression goes, "You can't kill a sucker." The idea simply is that "if you lose money in speculation you're incurable because you have a fresh incentive, namely, to "get even."

"Tens of thousands of people who for years have been reading the financial sections of the newspapers, but whose incomes were not sufficient to permit them to indulge in stock market speculation in rails and industrials, found in cheap electronics stocks the thing they were looking for... an opportunity with limited capital to give full play to their gambling or speculative instinct."

Most gamblers are not deterred by one, two, or even three losses in a row. "Is it not a habit of horse players when they lose five races in succession to make a plunge bet on the sixth with a view to getting even?"

There is no doubt that speculation and the lure of quick profits dominates humanity. There is solace in the relatively new safeguards set up by the Securities and Exchange Commission in 1933 and the latest investigation in 1963 which once again have added to the safeguards which protect the average investor. There is also a reasonable assurance of safety from speculative excesses by the controlling influence of the Federal Reserve Board which regulates the margin requirements of investors. Careful study of the state of speculation dictates the rise and fall of margin percentages. The current 70 percent will hold until the speculative tenor of the market causes it to be raised to 90 or 100 percent. (The current 50 percent has lasted for decades).

"The mercury of speculation has made fortunes for many, and caused the throbbing sadness of others. No one can expect to be a winner all the time, especially when dealing with low quality, highly speculative companies. There is a particularly gratifying feeling, however, in knowing firsthand of a new company which is about to explode into a new dynamic area with strong commercial possibilities. When the publicity spreads the story of your company's discovery, the public rushes in wildly to see what it can salvage in the way of profit."

Money should not lie idle... it should be working for you. See that you are careful to deploy it effectively... assure your own growth, profit, and well being by wisely managing its investment to your best advantage.

All quotations are taken from "My Adventures With Your Money" by George Graham Rice.

34) NOBODY LOSES

Intelligence, wisdom, pride, ego, and status are some of the reasons why people who invest in the stock market refuse to admit that their efforts to make money have met with failure. It is a standing joke around the boardrooms that, "nobody loses." We all know that this legend is not true. They take pains to inflate their successes. They want their friends to think that they are big operators ... the understanding being that big operators never lose in the market. That is another fiction.

People who are not easily taken in by excited talk are nevertheless aware of the unlimited opportunities which the stock market offers an individual. The fascination of the ebb and flow of market sentiment pits the mass of corporate potential against the foresight and knowledge of the investor. Those with a thorough understanding of the reasons for a sustained advance by a particular company can pyramid their success as the price gets higher and higher. It is also an ingredient of success to know when to take a profit, "stocks are made to sell." The timing of the sale can make the difference between profits and losses.

"When I buy on the way up, I change the direction of a stock," is the lament often heard by traders. It is therefore important to make lightning-like decisions to keep pace with investor sentiment.

The stock market has attained to such a high level of popularity that it has now become acceptable as a subject for parlor talk. Market experiences are also important conversational pieces at cocktail parties. Millions of new investors who are in the first flush of their interest in the market are eager to learn by reading the financial publications and hearing the experiences of others. The vagaries of the stock market are easier to take when they are in a vicarious form.

Anyone who has been bitten by the market bug realizes that this increasing interest is natural. There are many millions of others who are succumbing to the temptation of trying their skill in the world of corporate finance. Their first faltering steps must be guided by an understanding that the mine fields and booby traps could get them. If they are aware of the fact that participation in stock buying does not automatically entitle them to profits, they can avoid the disillusionment which many thousands of others have suffered.

Above all they must learn very early in their stock market career that it is a certainty that there are times when they will lose money. The sooner this happens, the more fortunate the investor will be. He can then use his sad and emotional experience as an example of what to avoid and what not to do in his quest for market profits. Moreover, he can then look askance at anyone who happens to say, even facetiously, "Nobody loses."

35) RUMORS AND GUARANTEES

There is an abundance of animation and excited talk in the many brokerage offices throughout the country. A great deal of what you hear is helpful and informative, but I'm afraid there will always be some really wild and loosely based rumors which find their way to the ears of the eager to learn novice. A novice is one who enthuses and believes the word of a complete stranger without the slightest thought of checking out the facts of as given situation. This person can be in the market for twenty years... if he takes things at face value, without allowing for the source of the story, or the obvious excitement and exaggeration of the teller... he is still a novice.

I am particularly wary of the person who is so sure he is right, that he is willing to give out guarantees... you know the type... he is not uncommon in the market. The sorry fact is that this person has missed his vocation, for with the unlimited supply of guarantees at his command, he should certainly have been a bigger success selling washing machines or television sets. The last guy I knew who bought a barrel of stock with a guarantee is now wearing that same barrel!

Would a person swallow a piece of steak without chewing it thoroughly? Yet in a situation which is a good deal more vital, and important to their financial well being, people swallow whole and unproved rumors and tell stories without seeking the guidance and counsel of experienced cool-headed advisors.

The New York Stock Exchange has been conducting an educational campaign for years to enlighten these new investors. It is being aided by many member houses who are using their own funds to warn against unwise speculation. Many a disappointed and disillusioned stockholder has left the market because he felt that he was taken. There is no reason why he should blame anyone but himself. No one twisted his arm... he made up his own mind to buy the stock. He held it when it started to go down. His own greed had him entranced... and his paralysis caused his trouble.

There is an urgent need for speculative capital to finance the industries of tomorrow. Yesterday's prime moving speculators created and fostered the Mining Industry and the Railroads. Today's speculators are the vital force behind the Electronics, Office machines, and space industries. This is no plea for a cessation of speculation... it is just another indictment of irresponsible investment... the kind that leads ti individual tragedy.

There are many speculative stocks in the quality class. There is no need to risk your money in a highly speculative company which is comparatively unknown, and therefore very thinly traded. The only time a stock rises is when there is a demand for it. How can there be a demand for a well hidden company.

We all know that speculation involves risk. We suffer that risk for the avowed purpose of making a profit. If some unwitting person is foolish enough to brag about a guarantee, ask him to put it in writing. You'll find how solid his guarantee is immediately. If you want guarantees of assured safety you can't find them in speculative stocks. You are not even certain of the results of an investment in "Blue chip" equities. Part of the excitement and fascination of stocks is the uncertainty of their direction. Be alert to the opportunity of learning how to find a special situation before the crowd rushes in. The ability to do this, in a variety of cases, will be your best guarantee of a profitable future in the stock market.

36) THE BARGAIN HUNTER

There is a particular type of individual in the stock market who is his own worst enemy. He constantly chooses to place buy orders below the market, and sell orders above the market. This type of person is commonly referred to as "A Bargain Hunter."

When he is all set to buy a stock, and it is selling at 11 1/2 , he will instruct his broker to buy it at 11. In many cases the stock will start moving up until it is out of range, and he will not buy it at all. If the stock goes down in price he lowers his bid price so that it seems as if he does not want to buy the stock at all, but wants to play around with orders which will never be executed.

The same thing happens when the bargain hunter wants to sell a stock. If the price of his stock is 35 ½ he will put in a sell order at 36. His rigidity and inflexibility can often cause disappointment. While the sell order languishes in the order room, good till cancel, the price of the stock settles down to 31. There might be some profit in the stock, but the likelihood is that a year or more of profit was lost by the hardheadedness of our greedy bargain hunter.

There is little sense in postponing a purchase once you've made a decision to buy. When valid reasons prompt you to buy a stock, it is foolish to hesitate. Don't let a fraction of a dollar keep you from your desire. Many investors have learned from bitter experience that it is usually smart to put in a market order when they want to buy. This is a purchase order at the best price once it reaches the floor of the exchange.

There is no bargain basement where one can find stocks at lower prices than they appear on the tape. Prices are always the result of the interplay of supply and demand. If the stock you want is selling off on the day you buy it, you will usually buy it lower. If it is in demand you will have to pay a premium. Don't expect to find sentiment in your favor at the exact moment you decide to buy or dell. If you are itching to buy a stock... buy it. Don't spend the next few months in anguish as the stock you liked climbs in the brisk manner you imagined it could. If it goes down you would certainly want to sell it. But a fast run-up after you pass up a market purchase is one of the many aggravating results of poor investment behavior.

The advice in this corner is to buy the stocks you like regardless of their price. If they are as sound as you believe, they will continue to rise. If you guess wrong, or some unexpected bad news causes the stock to retreat, don't look for a special price at which to sell. The bargain you seek is the company you are buying... not the particular price which you set for its purchase. Look for the good companies and they will become your bargains.

In the long run, those people who hunt for bargains in the way I've described will have a host of stories to tell their friends. Stories of how they missed buying good stocks because of their ignorance, stubbornness, or lack of common sense. The sad paradox will be that because of the bargains they hunted, their life will forever be haunted... by the many ifs and whys in the checkered past of their market career.

37) BAD LUCK

There are forces at work in the market which are intangible or abstract. They are at odds with the accepted rules and theories which are expanded with vehemence by veterans of the street. This shadowy uncontrollable something is luck.

"Some get it... some aint got it... and I aint got it." This expression which is the trademark of the well known comedian Jimmy Durante can well be the lament of thousands of investors throughout the country.

It is true that most investors, using the soundest principles of investment, have run into the most nerve-wracking and depressing experiences that are possible. Everyone who has put money into common stock has had these difficulties at some time or another. It is not uncommon to hear stories of people who have reached into the market bag and come up with a handful of aggravation.

"I know a man who has an uncanny knack of always picking a "loser," said one tape-watcher to his friend. "If he buys a stock, be sure that you sell it short," he continued.

"Does he pick these stocks on his own, or does he consult with someone?" insisted the friend.

"I don't know, but if he's using a Ouija board, he'd better throw it away... it's making him a pauper."

Upon closer investigation it was learned that every time this man bought a tobacco stock a cancer scare developed. When he bought a defense stock a disarmament conference was called. If he bought a drug stock the Senate called for an investigation of drug prices. At every turn he was clobbered with adverse publicity. It seems almost a pity that these things actually happen because so many thousands of investors suffer the consequences.

There is small consolation in knowing that you are not alone in your unhappy state. It would be easier to be mutually unhappy with the many thousands whose market profits force them to pay more income taxes. This is what we are all striving for, and there is always hope as long as the money holds out.

For those struggling millions who are losing money in the stock market it is helpful to know that the road to market success is not always a smooth one, but is often full of roadblocks and detours. Success has been achieved by many who were undeterred by disappointment, failure, and even despair.

Usually the interplay of market forces is responsible for the so-called luck of those fortunate winners. The fact is that people with good sense, foresight, perseverance, and patience will forge their own brand of luck, and with it, the long sought goal of stock market success.

38) THROWING GOOD MONEY AFTER BAD

There is a phrase in the stock market which says, "Don't throw good money after bad." The obvious meaning of this axiom is to refrain from purchasing additional quantities of a particular stock if the original lot has met with bad luck. This action is called averaging out.

There are differences of opinion with respect to this philosophy. Some people think that averaging is a short cut to the poorhouse. Others use it successfully to flatten out the peaks and valleys of the business cycle.

It is dangerous to average out an inactive stock. The popular and thinly traded stocks can aggravate the most patient investor. The best course of action with slow moving, out of favor is to sell them, not to buy more and put yourself into a deeper hole.

When you buy a quality stock at its peak price and it starts a long, painful decline, you owe it to yourself to get rid of it. This should be done before the loss gets out of hand. In many cases hesitant investors fail to rid themselves of stocks while they sink into a deeply depressed state. If you happen to find yourself in that position, and you judge that your stock has a negligible downside potential, employ the theory of contrary action. Buy more of your depressed stock at the lower price. You will be buying when most people are selling. If your stock is actively traded in normal times, you can look for a rebound when the tide turns. Good stocks do come back, and many times they go up faster than when they declined.

It is therefore not impossible to expect that success can be achieved by averaging out good stocks, and in truth we can coin a corollary to our original aphorism. It should read, "Sometimes good money can turn bad money into good money."

39) OUR BRILLIANT FUTURE

All eyes are on the tape. From the ten o'clock (nine-thirty now) bell to the close, America watches with anxious interest. For isn't this ticker tape the heart of our country's economy? Doesn't it define with clear mathematical precision the direction it is choosing?

It is interesting to observe the intense concentration which most tape watchers display. As they turn their heads from the ticker tape to the broad Dow Jones news ticker, they resemble a cobra which is swaying in a fixed trance to the tantalizing notes of the fakir's flute.

This interest is not hard to understand since the stock market is achieving a popularity of increasing proportions, and thousands of investors and speculators are joining the growing ranks every week. Trading has reached the point where the high speed tickers are now being developed to meet the expanding volume. Automatic quote machines are already a reality for busy registered representatives, and color tapes, greatly enlarged, will be in the boardrooms in the not too distant future. All that remains is for computers to predict the course of stock prices. That will make things easier for everybody.

The course of business is truly becoming a national concern. Everybody with a few dollars in the market is worried about strikes, court cases, and any foreign news which may affect the course of the market. News magazines, financial publications, and statistical advisory services are enjoying an unprecedented demand. In short there is now an interest in the stock market and an intelligent and enlightened public to go along with it.

Prognosticators of the past have consistently been cautious and timid in their predictions of the future. They have underestimated the force of America's greatness, and its live, vigorous forward march of progress. Even now we cannot conceive of the wonders which await us, and the opportunities they present.

We are on the threshold of the Space age. The vast unknown attacks the imagination with dynamic force. Are there inhabitable new worlds? Does intelligent life exist on the other planets? Science prepares to do battle with these and other questions, and American industry is there to see that the job is done. Investors and speculators will back those corporations with the capital that is needed to finance the research.

With this mammoth investment in the future, shareholders will continue to read the tape, look behind the headlines, and maintain an increasingly active interest in the movement of our country's economy. Not everyone will be able to maintain a vigil at the tape, but the urge to know the latest developments will wax greater in the months and years to come.

40) DECISIONS: RIGHT OR WRONG

The most important tool in your stock market kit would have to be a quick, decisive mind. The ability to make decisions is a valuable aid in everyday life... in Wall Street it is the difference between success and failure.

This does not mean that one who can make snap decisions will always be right. The chances are that he will be wrong many times. The fact is that in taking prompt action, there is always the possibility that he will be right. It is easier to do nothing when confronted with a situation that demands your attention. That is the lazy way which most of us take. Inaction leads to stagnation and failure. When we take no action, we are almost always wrong.

An examination of your stocks will remind you of the many times you chose inaction to decision. It will appear obvious that in a number of cases the courage of decision would have prevented you from being locked in with a loss too big to absorb.

All too often we buy a stock for a quick trade and wind up holding it for five years. In some cases, paying interest on the debit balance of our margin accounts.

How lackadaisical can we get when our precious money is involved? An objective should be inviolable and binding on our conscience. Profits are lost and losses are swollen by the indolent stock trader.

Be alert... get mad at yourself if you fail to keep a constant check on all your invested capital. Don't buy stocks, put them away, and forget about them. Buy them... watch them... and see that they perform as expected. If they don't ... sell them and buy others that will.

41) A SHORT PARADOX

A person sells a stock short because he firmly believes that he will be able to buy it a lower price sometime later and therefore make a profit. That is the plain and unembroidered fact about selling short. There is no secret about it... a long wants a stock to go up... a short wants it to go down.

For some inexplicable reason, a short seller has a different kind of stomach. He is scared from the moment his order is executed. For some strange reason there is a different feeling in a person who has bought a stock long and sees it go lower, and a short seller who sees his stock go higher. The long is not at all happy. He wants his stock to go higher so he can take a profit, but when it sells off he is patient and confident that it can come back. The short, on the other hand is scared at the outset. When his stock starts to rise a numbing fear sets in and changes his life into a nightmare.

The only reason one could have for shorting a fundamentally strong stock is that it has had an extended rise. Normally a reaction is due for profit taking and consolidation. Sometimes this reaction is long overdue, and the shorts and the shorts keep it from occurring.

In cases where a short position is very large, it becomes almost obvious that the price of the stock continues to climb because the shorts themselves are buying to cover their own sales. In other words, the fact that they were selling short was working against their goal of seeing the stock decline. They and their nervous colleagues could not stand the sight of their rising stock, and it was their buying which caused the rise.

Money is made on the short side of the market as well as the long. Don't make the mistake of shorting a stock just because it is high. Make sure the technical and fundamental position of the stock is weak. See that everything is in your favor. Then with your heart in your mouth, wait for your uptick.

42) MERGERS

"Oh, it's all right," said my friend with boyish delight, "Lanolin Plus is going to merge with Hazel bishop and it will go all the way up in price." This dialogue graphically illustrates the common fallacy of the inevitability of merger success.

The past decade can truly be called the era of mergers. In the last ten years there have been more corporate consolidations than there have been in the last one hundred years. There are valid reasons for the increase in recent years. Let us see why they have become so popular.

In the first place not every firm enters into merger talks because it wants to. Some companies are forced to in order to survive. This happens when increased competition and rising costs result in unmanageable losses for a small company. This condition makes it impossible for a firm to remain in business, but its tax position will make it desirable for acquisition by a larger company in the same field, or any company which has a large profit.

It is sometimes possible for the acquiring company to

save the whole cost of acquisition , whether it is cash, stock, or a combination of both... by means of the tax loss carry forward of the company which is purchased. Even if this does not happen, the new company can be integrated with little additional overhead, and its sales can be translated into profits instead of its former losses.

A second type of merger can be considered a defensive one, although its primary aim is to diversify and increase its net profit. This is a common occurrence in the aircraft and aerospace industries. The companies which have enjoyed a large amount of defense business, have not always had an equal amount of pleasure in contemplating their small amount of profit. Their ratio of sales to earnings is among the lowest of all industries. It is unfortunate for them that their business is so carefully scrutinized by this government although it is the duty of the Pentagon to protect the taxpayer's money and see that we get the most for our defense dollars.. Renegotiation of contracts and other aggravating defense procedures have made the defense business a hazardous one. It is true that there are new incentives for defense producers in cost-plus fixed-fee contracts, which enable companies to reap the advantage of efficiency and cost-cutting procedures.

More recently our Secretary of Defense McNamara has put forth a plan whereby our important defense contractors will be able to increase their profit margins. It is imperative that incentives be increased or the technical skill of our country's prime defense contractors will be diverted to the more lucrative area of the commercial field outside of defense.

It has become a matter of necessity, however, for companies whose main source of business is the Federal Government, to actively seek a marriage with non-defense firms which have a higher ratio earnings to sales There have been three such mergers in the recent past of prominent defense companies: General Dynamics and Material Service, Boeing Company and Vertical Aircraft, and Martin company and American Marietta. The earnings of the merged companies should eventually be improved due to the addition of their stable and highly profitable subsidiaries.

The third and most common type of merger involves two companies in the same field who wish to benefit from a union of operations. The savings in costs may result in more net profit from a like amount of sales. It is generally the larger of the two which remains as the successor company. In many cases these mergers are consummated to expand product lines, and in some cases they are blocked or held up by the Justice department when consolidation of the two companies tend toward monopoly or restraint of trade.

The three major classes of mergers have been examined here, and to summarize, they are the following: 1. The tax loss merger. 2. The diversification merger. 3. The merger to complement product lines and reduce total overhead.

All mergers are initiated for the purpose of achieving more profits. In many cases the validity of the reasons for the union are borne out in the subsequent success of the new company. However, the word merger is not a magic formula for increased profits. Many mergers are launched with increased amounts of stock, additional directors, and other forms of added overhead or dilution of equity. With adverse fortune a merged company can experience poor sales and earnings just as the companies would have done in the same circumstances if no marriage took place. Merged companies were not immune to bad news!

I therefore take exception to the prevailing myth that all mergers must lead to success. Each one must be evaluated on its own merits. If a merger of two companies appears imminent, and its success seems assured, I can understand an investor's confidence. I deplore, with good reason, the generalizations which unwisely put a halo on all companies which enter into preliminary discussions toward a possible union.

43) THE CHALLENGE

If the pessimists and doubters were right, man would still be following the plow. History has shown that vision, imagination, and courage can overcome the derision and cynicism of the people. Such was the faith of those rugged individuals who fearlessly forged new industries, built great cities, and served our country through years of trial and pain... years of famine and pestilence... peace and war... struggle and growth.

Woven deep into the fabric of America is the strength and power of its free enterprise system. Many are the inspiring stories of success which attended the growth of the massive industries that support our country's economic and military needs. Today, as in the recent past, new areas of adventure and growth await the men who have the courage to accept the challenge.

Man is at the threshold of new discoveries. The moon, the planets, and the stars of our solar system are no longer out of reach. Tomorrow, the breakthroughs into cosmic space will be a reality. The extent of human progress is bound only by our imagination, and science is gradually exceeding these limits.

Every generation has cautiously underestimated man's potential for growth and progress, and ours is no exception.. The dreamed of wonders await the unborn generations of the future. When the historians of the 25th century look back to our period, they will no doubt feel that 20th century man was too cautious in his attempt to probe the unknowns of the universe.

Living on the planetoids of our solar system, with the accumulated knowledge of five additional centuries, the man of the future will have conquered all disease, and found the answer to longevity. Interstellar travel will be common. With all this and more at his command, it would seem to us that progress will no longer be necessary. That will not be the case, because the vastness of space will offer unlimited areas for adventure and exploration.

The sum of all these years of advances will prove that those things which were called impossible in our time, will be as outmoded and obsolete as the spinning wheel, in that far off wonderful future.

44) THE MARKET LETTER

One of the most well known quotes in the stock market is J.P. Morgan's answer to inquiries on the probability of the market's movement. He simply and straightforwardly said, "It will fluctuate." Now that may seem like a planned evasion, but it is undoubtedly a good reply, and one which leaves little chance for recourse by the questioner.

There is an abundance of advice available to a prospective stockholder. Most of it is the result of painstaking research from the collective brains of experts. However, there is nothing absolute in the stock market, since so many eventualities can exert unfavorable pressure on the direction of stock prices. Among the most distressing of these are strikes, Federal investigations, price cuts, new competition in the same field, increasing overhead costs, and the threat of war and its unsettling effects on the economy.

For this reason the market expert, the financial columnist, and the research specialist must be a master of semantics. His exposition must be couched in such an indecisive manner as to afford him an escape hatch should his recommendation fail to perform. Here is an example of the ambiguity which can be found in any market letter. I invented this analysis using the key words which are common to all such reports.

"Although recent market action has been less than dynamic, we believe that the uncertainties of the last few weeks were characterized by drift and skepticism will change in the immediate future. While we wouldn't rush in until the present liquidation is over, it is a distinct possibility that a modest rise in equities will replace the cross-currents and doubt which have been depressing a major portion of the list."

It is obvious from the foregoing example that market letters bear a strong resemblance to weather reports. The cautious language of both includes such indefinite words as possible, varied, unsettled, likely, etc. This is hardly an attempt to equate the prediction of stock prices and the weather, although some people might argue the point affirmatively.

There are many ways to learn about the operations of a company. The easiest and most accurate indicator of a corporation's possibilities for future growth is its past history of sales and earnings. Performance measures a company's worth. A solid record of increasing growth for a period of five to ten years should be proof positive that a trend is in progress. However, there is no guarantee that this is so, and there are enough examples to prove that growth trends can be reversed.

The net effect of this discussion is that prediction of stock prices is at best a difficult and uncertain task. Those who read analyses, research reports, and the like, must realize that they are written by mortals. They are not seers and prophets. The facts they report are true but the projections are subject to the vicissitudes of all business.

If one uses the information as a guide, and not something to live and die with, he will fare more successfully in the investment field. When a research prediction runs into some unforeseen difficulty, even the writer would agree that the original conclusions will not be realized.

There is no short cut to success in the market, and there are no sure things. Market analysts give us insight into situations through their careful research, but all investments must be followed closely to see if expected earnings materialize. With the proper attitude toward this research, and an intelligent, decisive approach to price variations, market success can be realized.

45) DON'T FORGET ABOUT IT

Everyone has heard the expression-"Buy that stock, put it away, and forget about it!" This advice is usually given free of charge. The reason is obvious. Why should anyone invest a sum of money and promptly forget about it. On the contrary, it is advisable to keep a constant check on your holdings to see if they are meeting their intended objectives.

When you buy a blue chip stock, it is generally held for a longer period than a short term risk type situation. The painful truth is that in many cases when a stock is bought for attempt at a short term trade, the buyer forgets his objective and is stuck or "locked in" with a speculative stock, which doesn't pay a dividend, and has nosedived too long to know any other direction. It is safe to say that this type of person would be well advised to stay away from the more risky stocks and buy those which promise growth or secure income. In that way his investment will at least have a good chance of bearing fruit. In sum, it would not be amiss to tell a friend, "Buy that stock, put it away, but never forget about it!"

46) THE PSYCHOLOGICAL INFLUENCE

Everyone connected with the stock market should be aware of the factors, however slight, which affect the course of stock prices. They certainly should be conscious of the fundamental and underlying reasons for the market's direction.

In the broad sense, the sentiment of investors can be swayed by technical or psychological forces. Let us see what this means. The technical reason for a stock's action depends on the past history of its price movement. When a stock makes a new high, it will almost always bring in a flood of new orders. This influx of buying demand is usually market orders, and therefore the stock continues to go higher in price.

The psychological influence on the market is substantial, but in most cases it depends on a good fundamental and technical position. When these conditions exist, and the market is at a standstill, even the so-called experts begin to doubt their convictions. It is then that a turn for the better stands out against the background of a dull market.

When Korvette started its dramatic climb in 1961, it

was a tar to which all retailers hitched their wagon. Everybody went discount happy. The furor and excitement that attended its rise opened the eyes of even the most conservative elements in the merchandise section of the market. It put them in the unpopular and degrading position of a follower instead of a leader in the field. However, the dictates of good business caused them to scurry into discounting with all due haste. They had already lost some ground to the upstarts, and there was no use losing more because the idea was not original.

The above example shows how a dynamic stock can initiate the movement of a whole industrial group. There are other occasions when a varied group of stocks will take off on expanded volume. Eager tape-watchers who are always on the lookout for quick moving stocks jump at the opportunity of joining a newly formed bandwagon. In the wake of these alert market operators, the broad mass of the buying public pours its money into these new, fast moving stars.

A feeling of urgency and excitement is created by this strong upside volume, and in many cases the general market follows with a broadly based advance. Thus we see how quickly market psychology can develop an exciting, emotional, and bullish movement. Sometimes these moves are short lived, when prevailing conditions are good the uptrend can be sustained.

The fact that sentiment and psychology are factors in the market's movement has been proven many times. However, this form of buying stock is subject to the danger of miscalculation and poor timing. Too many people buy their stock at the top of a move and sadly and disconsolately wait for a return to its purchase price.

In sum, it is not enough to know that the market is subject to emotional bursts of enthusiasm which give it force and vitality. Astute traders who carefully study the mood of the market may profit from these timely gyrations, but the average investor hasn't the sophistication or mature market skill to afford the risk. It is therefore important for him to understand that it is the basic quality of a company which determines its value and argues for its purchase.

47) CHARTS OR FUNDEMENTALS

There are two separate and distinct ways of analyzing stocks and their prices. These two approaches are called the Fundamental and the Technical. Each one has its own market and is useful for its particular stock market follower. It depends on his purposes and objectives in the market. Short term traders use the technical approach, and long term investors use the fundamental.

Fundamental analysis covers the broad spectrum of basic research and all which that implies...balance sheets, assets, liabilities, the many ratios which measure the quality of management, the dividend record, and the growth rate are some of the numerous standards which are used by analysts to rate a company within its own industry. Of course, one of the most important considerations is the company's earnings.

If a comprehensive review of the company's history suggests that it is a worthwhile recommendation, it is basically an intermediate to long term selection. This can mean anywhere from six months to a couple of years. For this reason unpredictable occurrences may negate the excellence of a very thorough research effort. Unfortunately stock picking must continue to be the inexact science it is despite constant analysis by trained personnel with access to company information. Many predictions based on research do work out, it is this searching examination of a company and what makes it tick that is the best method of determining where the price of the stock is headed. What happens later is uncontrollable. Infringements, accidents, cancellation of contracts, and loss of key personnel are only a few of the things which alter the smooth flow of corporate progress

Technical analysis is the art of chart reading, and the analysis of the various averages and indices which market followers cherish. It has nothing to do with the company. It doesn't matter if the company makes marbles or ball bearings, the technician is strictly concerned with the market action of the company's stock, and the volume of its shares traded. In the course of a chartist's analysis he deals with pennants, flags, head and shoulders formations, necklines, triplr bottoms and tops, and many other chart patterns. He also seeks to analyze the interaction and comparison of the Dow Jones Averages, Standard and Poor's 500 Stock Index, the advance Decline Line, Odd-Lot Indices, Lowrey's Buying power and Selling Pressure Lines, and Barron's Confidence Index, etc. The study of chart reading is complex and several books have been written on the subject. By simply explaining the chart action of any company, a technician is able to forecast with a fair degree of accuracy where the price of a stock will meet a resistance or support area, and when a breakthrough will occur, or where the price will go before it meets further trouble.

It should now be fairly obvious why the short term trader is more apt to use charts and the technical approach and the long term investor the fundamental. While neither form of analysis is infallible, it is the best means we have of helping ourselves through the maze of stock market data. It must be understood that the sensitivity of stock prices to every piece of news whether national, international, political, or psychological can play havoc with any forecast or interpretation. This uncertainty lies at the heart of the fascination which buying common stocks has for people all over the world.

48) SELLING SHORT

Selling short is one phase of stock market activity which has long been the private domain of the floor trader. Recently, many new people have jumped on the bandwagon and have used the volatility of the market to sell short and make some money. They are quick to admit that they did not fully understand the mechanics of short selling. All they know was that you sold short today and the next day you already had a profit. It was much quicker than making a profit in a Bull Market, so they told all their friends, and the short interest soared to a new high.

The practice of selling short is simply the sale of borrowed stock with the intention of replacing it sometime in the future at a lower price. If the stock is bought in a t a lower price the short seller realizes a profit. If the price of the stock,, he will sustain a loss. A high short interest in any given stock is a bullish indication since every share which is sold short must inevitably be bought and replaced. This potential buying demand can cause a sharp rise in the price of the stock.

In a surging, growing, and expanding economy it can prove fatal to be a pessimist for too long a time. There is no limit to the price of a stock on the way up. Your broker can persuade you to limit your loss with the placement of a buy-stop order above the price at which you sold short. Most Americans are optimistic and would prefer to buy long. In fact, those who do sell short usually cover too soon, even if the stock is going down and their profit is increasing. People just don't feel the same when they are betting against a stock.

It is true that the stock market can go two ways. However, large profits were made in 2008 when stock prices melted. The selling fed on itself, and a flood of stock was offered to the few staunch buyers who had the foresight to see beyond the panic. Their faith in the future of our economy was generously rewarded.

As a Bear Market develops, short selling picks up in intensity until it assumes enormous proportions. This high short interest prevails when stock prices are hitting bottom. When a change in sentiment is suspected, important buying will move prices up. Then the worried shorts will rush to cover their short sales for fear that the rise in prices will widen their losses or narrow their profits. This short covering coupled with bargain hunting and other new buying can create a demand which it is too great for the sellers to satisfy. This marks the beginning of a new trend, and the emotions can become just as strong in the other direction.

49) THE STOCK CERTIFICATE

There is a satisfying feeling of ownership which comes with the delivery of that ornately designed and important looking certificate that denotes part ownership of a corporation. The fact that it takes a couple of weeks to receive this stock certificate seems to bother many people, since they have already paid in full... they can't understand why they have to wait so long for that cherished piece of paper. It becomes further complicated when a dividend is paid while the stock is still in "street" name.

All stock is bought and sold on the floor of the various exchanges by representatives of the many member houses, and the securities are credited to their particular firm at the Stock Clearing Corporation. There is no question about the owner... if you buy 100 shares of General Motors on a particular date, you are the beneficial owner as of that date and are entitled to all dividends which are declared from that day on. It would just be impossible to have stock bought on the floor of the New York Stock Exchange in the name of the many thousands of individuals who buy and sell stock every day.

Once the stock is bought and paid for (there is a five business day period between the purchase and the settlement date), the holder may then decide whether he wants it held in the name of his broker, or transferred to his name and shipped to his home. Many people cannot experience the true feeling of possession unless they have the stock in their own bank vault.

If a stockholder decides to leave his stock in safekeeping, most Wall Street houses will hold it in his account without charge, and send monthly statements which record all the transactions which take place during the preceding month. Purchases, sales, dividends are shown in either a cash or margin account, with automatic dividend disbursement if the account so desires.

In the event that a stockholder wants his certificate delivered, his broker issues instructions after the settlement date to have the stock transferred and shipped. It is then approved by the proper department and the shares are sent to the transfer agent of that particular company. The transfer agent issues a new certificate for the same number of shares represented by the old certificate, which is then cancelled. A proper record of the transaction is made and then the old and new certificates go to the registrar.

The registrar is solely concerned with making certain

that the number of new shares is exactly the same as the old shares cancelled. After registration, the stock goes back to the transfer agent.

The new certificate is then mailed to the stockholder, and from that time on, all dividends and company correspondence are sent directly to his address. This whole procedure normally takes ten days to two weeks after approval, unless the volume of trading on the stock market is unusually high and there is a large backlog of work at the transfer agent.

The next time you buy a stock, leave your instructions with your broker... in that way there will be no delay in receiving those certificates which colorfully tell the world that you are a part owner of corporate America.

50) WHEN TO BUY AND SELL

One of the most difficult decisions which faces a stockholder is when to sell a given holding. It rivals in importance the problem's counterpart of when to buy. This dilemma is aptly posed by an age old axiom of the market, "When to buy and sell is more important than what to buy and sell."

Let us examine this adage carefully and see what one should do when faced with the particular problem that it points out. Bear in mind that this question is equally difficult whether you are taking a profit or a loss. I do feel however, that it is normally more difficult for most people to take a loss than it is to take a profit. That doesn't make it easy to take a profit.

If you must narrow things down to a formula, it would seem that your decision should be based on your objective. Everyone who enters the stock market intelligently should decide in advance of his entry if he is interested in long term growth, income, or risk type securities.

It is easy to comprehend that the only problem involved to the first category is trying to pick a growth stock at a time when it is not selling at a prohibitive price times earnings ratio. Nobody can be lucky enough to find the bottom, but there are times when good growth stocks are depressed.

When does one sell a growth stock? Well if long term growth was the objective it would obviate the problem of deciding. One would obviously hold for many years so that the full potential of the company's growth may be realized. There will be reactions and sell-offs, but for a true Growth Stock the trend should always be up. That goes for sales, earnings, and market price. If you find a drop in sales or earnings, you no longer have a growth stock and it is time to look for another place to put your money. In other words , the only time to sell a growth stock is when it stops growing, or when your objective changes.

When should you buy an Income Stock? Simple... whem it is paying the rate which you are looking for. There is no reason to sell unless the dividend is cut or eliminated. In this category there is no special problem or difficulty. Most income seekers are content to hold their stocks as long as they continue to get liberal dividends. They are even unmoved by a drop in the market price of their stocks, for they feel that the yield will eventually attract enough new money to send the price back to the level of their purchase.

The last category of stocks is undoubtedly the reason for the birth of our problem, for this type of stock belongs only in risk accounts. This risk may lead to profits or losses and these give rise to the need for decision.

No rule works all the time. The market will often do the unexpected and catch an investor by surprise. While it is advisable to hold Growth and Income securities for long periods of time, it is a common error to hold a speculative stock long past the point where all hope is gone for the fulfillment of the promise which induced its purchase. A short term trader should be just what his name implies. He should be willing to take losses when his stock does not perform as expected. He should also accept a reasonable profit and be constantly alert for new opportunities. The trader must be decisive, forward looking, and he should never look back with regret, but try to learn from his experiences. Above all the astute short term trader must set his goals and stick by them.

If he decides to accept a profit of ten percent on his investment, he should be satisfied with it and not look for more. If he has to accept a similar loss, it is only because he must continue to retain his vital buying power.

Emotion ruins the investor. Hope and greed are in a constant struggle with reason. The seasoned market follower knows that stocks which have good value are good buys when they are depressed and the market looks its worst.

Unfortunately, a larger proportion are subject to the heat of emotional waves of buying, and seem to buy at a time when stocks have had a sustained rise and are near their top. Maturity in the art of investing for our seasoned trader has reached its high mark when he is taking a profit on securities he bought when they were undervalued in a depressed market. He is selling to those eager buyers who need a surging market to prod them into action. Of course the stock is now fully priced, and while a profit is delightful, it cannot obscure the task which lies ahead of this successful trader... the job of finding the next situation which will yield the same result.

51) TIMING

There is a mild difference of opinion among the minions of Wall Street on the question of when is the best time to buy stocks. N the broad sense the disagreement stems from a conviction on the part of many people that the right way to buy is when a stock is on its way down, or as the expression goes, "bottoming out." The other school of buyers maintains that it is best to buy when a stock is on the way up. There is no clearly defined answer to this problem, and it will remain with us as long as stocks are traded. The best we can do here is to point out from the experience of others what causes the rise and fall of stocks, and in that way we may arrive at a considered conclusion about the timing of our purchases.

There are a multitude of reasons why a stock is depressed and making new lows. The main reason is the lack of good earnings, poor sales, and the cutting or omission of dividends. The object of researchers and bargain hunters alike is to find a sleeper. This can be a quality company in a depressed state of sales and earnings. If they discover such a company early enough they have found something worthwhile. This group of people is constantly alert to the action of stocks as they make new lows every day. It is unfortunate that one cannot know the exact bottom price of a stock as it slides consistently to new lows, but that does not matter if you have really found a plum that is ripe for the picking.

The latent value of your discovery can make it climb as far as its potential will allow. There investors look beyond the current struggles of a company... a bad strike for example, or if it is harried by expenses for new product development. They know that the force of a company's quality, stability, and unquestioned earning power will inevitably send the price of the stock back to more respectable levels.

The other group of investors is undoubtedly a larger one. I say this in the belief that most people are attracted to a stock when it is behaving well and making new highs. In those cases it is usually better earnings and the expectation of good news in the form of a stock split or increased dividends or both which causes a stock to continue rising. Growth stocks behave this way, and it is as difficult to guess how high a stock is going to rise before "topping out" as it is to know how low it will go before "bottoming out."

The air of uncertainty which attends these problems makes the selection of stocks the inexact science it is. This compounds the wonder and fascination of the stock market. Just think how dull it would be if we knew exactly what was going to happen every time we bought a stock? The doubt about the outcome of an investment multiplies the elation when you finally do hit upon a winner. When that happens you have a new and intriguing problem... when is the right time to sell?

52) DIVERSIFICATION

One of the cardinal principles of sound investing is to have a diversified portfolio. The usual tragedy for most people is they have far less than one would consider a portfolio, and that their diversified group of stocks is nothing but a hodge podge of stocks which have been accumulated through the years upon the advice of well-intentioned friends, hot tips which have a habit of cooling off, and unsuccessful hunmches.

It is difficult to understand the inertia which paralyzes investors whose money has lain dormant in inactive stocks. They sit idly by and painfully watch the dynamic new favorites capture the headlines every day. If sufficient time has passed since the purchase of a stock, and it hasn't performed, sell it and put the money into something else. Most people are reluctant to take a loss. They wait an unlimited amount of time in an attempt to recover every nickel of their investment. This is a mistake because the loss of time may prove valuable in another stock... one

which is making a spectacular move.

The essentials should change with age. The following

recommendations offer in a general way a portfolio plan for the various investors:

The average mix of holdings for a young man should be strongly weighted with growth stocks. It should include some income producers for new investment reserves, and a small percentage of quality stocks with the added potential for capital appreciation.

The middle-aged person, man or woman, should retain half of his or her money in quality growth issues. The other half should be liberally dotted with income stocks, safe blue chips, and defensive issues. Speculative stocks in these portfolios should be left up to the individual.

When a person reaches retirement age, he is usually interested in income and safety. He does not want to risk money. He needs all the income he can get to supplement his social security and other forms of income. For this group of investors no growth stocks are recommended unless they offer income and safety as well. This is a difficult type to find because few growth stocks offer income. For the most part the utilities, tobaccos, food stocks, and other defensive issues should make up these portfolios. No speculation is called for. The balance of the investment should consist of dividend paying blue chips.

This a brief review of the average requirements for persons in the various groups of investors. It should be understood that there are always exceptions in individual cases. These problems are the responsibility of a financial advisor if he is the sole custodian of an investor. The goals should be decided at the outset, and when an investor attempts to leave the road toward that goal, he should be admonished by his broker.

The adoption of a well-planned program by an investor and a financial advisor, and the strict adherence to its step-by-step execution, is the intelligent way to a successful foray into the stock market. Without a professionally planned beginning and a portfolio revision and weeding of your stock garden, you can't seriously expect to have more than that same potpourri, to which people frequently refer to as your "well diversified portfolio."

53) THE LEGACY

One of the truly great heroes in the 200 year history of Wall Street is Gerald M. Loeb. G.M., as he was affectionately called by his close friends, was a partner in the investment firm of E.F. Hutton for most of his more than 50 years on Wall Street. His syndicated column was well-known to millions in the investment world, and so were his iconoclastic views. His most valuable contribution to the literature of the stock market is his best-selling book, "The Battle for Investment survival, which has sold millions of copies in several editions since it was first published in 1935. The book consists of a collection of articles that were originally published in Barron's, the financial weekly published by Dow Jones, which also owns the Wall Street Journal.

Many of the investment techniques successfully endured over the years by Loeb are at the heart of the method that built equity rapidly for six courageous investors who will be detailed in this book. The system is definitely not for the faint of heart, as you will see. Leverage works both ways. Loeb's maxims have withstood the test of time. The following are just a few of the direct quotes from his book that apply ro this work. They are only a small sample of the veritable gold mine of stock market wisdom that "The Battle for Investment Survival" contains:

The goal must be a speculative one, for only there lies safety, paradoxical as that may seem.

One should strive for a long profit on a small commitment.

Over-diversification is undesirable. One or two, or at most three or four equities should be bought.

Losses should be cut. They must be cut quickly, long before they become of any financial consequence.

The primary factor in securing market profits lies in sensing the general trend.

The right way to do it is to pyramid.

Stocks that are high and going higher are a good bet.

The intelligent and safe way to handle capital is to concentrate.

The greatest safety lies in putting all your eggs in one basket and watching the basket.

The sum of Loeb's stock market strategy therefore is to concentrate in a few stocks, buy them when they are in an uptrend, stay with them on the way up, sell them when they falter, and use a drop of 10 to 15 percent as a rule of thumb for selling out your position. The theme of this book is strongly related to these views, with the additional leverage that a margin account can bring to an investment position. That is one of the most important reasons why you can quickly multiply the value of your account. The speculative risk is always there whether you are on margin or you buy for cash. If your stocks go down and prove that you were wrong, sell them. The fear of margin is unwarranted as some of the historical facts will soon prove. This does not mean that as sharply falling market can melt your equity and bring on sleepless nights if you don't sell in a hurry. Loeb may not have recommended margin for his clients, but he was a veteran of the sharp selloff in 1929 and the early 1930s, which saw the Dow Jones Industrial Average sink to 42. "The Wizard of Wall Street" as his biography by Ralph G. martin was titled, has left a legacy for Wall Street. We shall see how the application of these principles actually works in the marketplace.

Excerpted from "Margin Power"

By Sheldon Zerden

54) ROTTEN FRUIT

For the first time in 76 years the most widely followed stock market barometer, the Dow Jones Industrial average has moved over 1000.(it has now exceeded 1,800 in 2014). It did so Tuesday, November 14th when it held a six point gain and closed at 1003.16. Wall Street has every reason to rejoice now that his important psychological barrier has finally been breached. But what does this historic event mean to the average stockholder? We must understand that the average consists of only 30 of the more than 2,000 companies listed on the New York Stock Exchange. Many hundreds of stocks have not even approached their highs of the past five or ten years, and at least 60 percent of the stocks in the Dow are no higher than they were in 1966 when the average last touched the 1000 mark.

This fact clearly points out the often expressed truth that the stock market is a market of stocks and must be approached with a great deal of selectivity. Most [people can't buy the average and their task is to buy those stocks which offer the best chance for appreciation. Once a decision is made and a stock is purchased it must be constantly watched for its expected rise. Don't let emotion anchor you into a losing situation.

Perhaps the technical analyst or chartist has the right idea. He follows the action of a stock, its price, volume, and pattern. He buys only when a stock shows to advantage and when it breaks down he sells without emotion or remorse. Remember- there are only two kinds of stocks-good and bad. Those that go up are good and those that go down are bad.

For those people who are holding bad stocks this writer has one bit of advice. Prune your stock garden as you would the dead leaves from a tree. Look in your refrigerator and discard the rotten fruit. A stock is only worth what someone is willing to pay for it now! It is no longer worth what you paid for it in the distant past.

In sum, the new Dow Jones Industrial Average record should spotlight the dilemma of the little guy who has been out of the stock market since 1968. The lesson to be learned is this- sell your bad stocks and buy the good ones. It is possible to share in the rewards of a rising stock market if you are selective and exercise the vigilance necessary to develop into a winner.

ABOUT THE AUTHOR

Sheldon Zerden is a veteran of over 40 years as a financial consultant, portfolio manager with Prudential Securities, which is now Wells Fargo. He has written financial columns for several financial publications and is the award-winning author of "Best Books on the Stock Market" He has recently published "The Wall Street Hall of Fame" and "Stock Market Wisdom" which are on Amazon.

He is married and has two daughters and three grandchildren.

www.ingramcontent.com/pod-product-compliance
Lightning Source LLC
Chambersburg PA
CBHW051506170526
45166CB00001B/410